PRAISE FOR
THE OTHER MAN DOWN

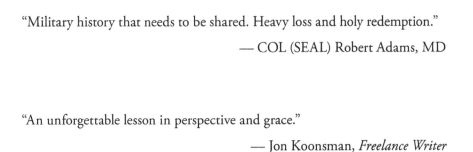

"Military history that needs to be shared. Heavy loss and holy redemption."

— COL (SEAL) Robert Adams, MD

"An unforgettable lesson in perspective and grace."

— Jon Koonsman, *Freelance Writer*

"Chad Littlefield was not the 'American Sniper,' but he was a hero to his mother nonetheless. This book recounts his death alongside Chris Kyle, and a mother's journey to and through grief. Riveting. A must read."

— Cmdr. Jeffrey L. Seif, *Dallas College / Police Academy*

The Other Man Down

A Mother's Journey After the
'American Sniper' Tragedy

BY
JUDY E. LITTLEFIELD

WRITTEN WITH ANGIE McEACHERN TODD

THE OTHER MAN DOWN:

A Mother's Journey After the 'American Sniper' Tragedy

Copyright © 2020 Judy E. Littlefield

First Edition

Published by Tactical 16, LLC
Monument, CO

ISBN: 978-1-943226-48-1 (paperback)

Dedicated to my husband and best friend Don, the wind beneath my wings. Also to my son Jerry, who has been my support and great source of encouragement from the beginning.

CONTENTS

Chapter 1

The Nightmare Began

"This is Taya Kyle," the voice on the other end of the phone said with intensity in her tone. "You need to bring Judy and come over to my house… There's been an accident."

I sat quietly, watching, and listening to Don as he questioned, "What happened?"

Taya replied quickly and firmly, "You need to get your wife and come over here."

Don's mind raced to remember exactly where the Kyles lived, "I know the street, but I don't know which house yours is."

"You can't miss it. There is law enforcement everywhere. What kind of car do you drive? There is a two block police perimeter around the house," Taya said.

"A blue Equinox. We're on our way," Don answered.

"Okay."

What would unfold to us over the few next hours and days became a nightmare from which we would not awaken.

It had been a typical Saturday night for us. We were already into our bedtime routine, preparing for church on Sunday. After a beautiful February day with the sun shining and the wind blowing, there was a little chill in the air.

The mailman had delivered a long-awaited piece of news that an inheritance we had been waiting on was finally on its way. I had texted our younger son, Chad, to share the good news with him. He was always kidding with us and asked if we needed his bank account number, "to deposit some unexpected funds, lol." Chad also let us know he and Chris were headed to the shooting range in Glen Rose, Texas. They were picking up a Marine who was struggling and needed to get out for the day.

Oh, how that text exchange would become immortalized as that evening came like a wrecking ball through the walls of our secure little world.

We backed out of our garage into the dark and drove anxiously to Chris and Taya Kyle's home. Although the Kyles had recently become well known because of Chris' best-selling book, *American Sniper*, our acquaintance with them had been pretty ordinary. We had gotten to know them sitting out at the soccer fields watching their daughter and our granddaughter play ball together.

Since that time, Chris and Taya Kyle had become celebrity status names, but to us, in that moment, they were dear friends to our beloved son and his family. So, when Taya said, "You need to get your wife and come over here…there's been an accident," my mind locked in on one scenario.

Was there some kind of accident in the truck? Were the guys stuck somewhere and they needed someone to come help pull them out of a ditch? What kind of accident?

We had our scares with accidents before, too.

Once when Chad was in high school, I was working the concession stand and Don was watching the football game from the stands. Another team mom came rushing to find me, saying that Chad was lying on the field waiting for an ambulance. They could not remove his helmet for fear of risk to his neck, which might have been broken.

As I captured Chad in my sight from quite a distance, I remember thinking he looked so big. The paramedics lifted him onto a backboard and loaded him into the ambulance. I was allowed to ride in the front, and I can remember looking into the back to see if he was all right, but I was unable to tell what was going on. Don followed behind in our car. We went in and waited for the scans and x-rays, sitting helplessly alone and anxiously waiting to be given some news, any news, but praying for good news.

Coaches and teammates eventually filled in all around us, praying and just doing what football teams do. They huddled up. When we finally got word that his injuries were far less significant than the coaches first thought, we were ecstatic. He was really bruised up, but he had not received any permanent damage to his neck or spine. We were so grateful, and we felt like he had really dodged a bullet.

The winding country roads were dark as Don and I traveled to the Kyles' home. As we reached their subdivision, we came to the police barricade. Apparently the police expected us based upon the description of our vehicle, because they opened the barricades for us readily.

I said, "We are the Littlefields."

The officer told us, "Chris has been injured, but we don't know about Chad."

I was taken aback that he knew Chad's name.

We found a spot to park in the already crowded street, got out of our car and walked hand-in-hand toward their house. There were law enforcement officers of every kind huddled all around, and we were directed by some to enter the house through the garage.

When we walked into the kitchen, we were met by our daughter-in-law. She told us Chris Kyle had been shot but that there was no word on Chad yet. She quickly rejoined her parents in the next room. We were dumbfounded.

Taya came into the room briefly. She let us know that if there was anything we needed we could ask just about anyone standing around. The house was peppered with Navy SEALs and police officers.

We stood there feeling alone, confused, and numb all at once. I asked one of the guys where I might find a waste basket to throw away my chewing gum, and he held out his bare hand and took my discarded gum. After that, I did ask for some water and I was given a glass full of water that was sitting on the countertop. For a moment I wondered if it already belonged to someone, but in light of everything, that hardly seemed important.

Everything was such a haze and yet somehow seemed so detailed at the same time. It was like I was watching a movie filled with characters, sights, and sounds all around me, but I was in the movie, too. Surreal, and yet so real.

At some point I knew that Chris had not just been shot but that he had been killed. I don't know how or when my understanding changed. I suppose we were in shock already, or at the very least we were thoroughly confused.

I remember that my cell phone began to ring, and text messages began pinging in. Our older son, Jerry, and our grandson, Colten, were trying desperately to reach us. Colten was very close to his uncle Chad. When Jerry found out that he was going to have a boy, he talked at length to Chad about a name. Chad had said that he always liked the name Colten, and Jerry agreed that should be the name for his son. So, there was a close attachment between Colten and Uncle Chad. Unbeknownst to us, the story was ablaze on the news on TV, and Jerry and Colten urgently wanted answers about Chad. The texts kept popping up on my phone screen.

"Is Chad okay?"

"Is Chad okay?"

"Is Chad okay?"

I was so confused and baffled by their questions. We hadn't told anyone yet about all that was happening, and still they were calling and texting relentlessly. Don and I sat alone together in a dimly lit room for what seemed like hours as twenty or more random strangers moved about.

Then a figured appeared before us. We later learned that he was a captain from the Midlothian Police Department. He stepped directly before Don and me. I remember feeling as though this officer was communicating with compassion, although I cannot say how except that he spoke in almost a whisper, telling us then that the other body found at the gun range was, in fact, Chad. He had been *murdered*.

I kept replaying the text messages and phone calls from Jerry and Colten asking, *"Is Chad okay?"* and how I had been told of other emergencies over the years and how Chad had always come out okay. Chad had been okay in football emergencies after being carried away in a neck brace on a stretcher and other life-threatening incidents, so I had just believed this would be the same.

I kept waiting on that feeling to come. I wanted someone to walk in the room and tell me things weren't as bad as they first thought. I wanted someone to tell me he was going to be okay.

Things started getting fuzzy after that, and I vaguely remember screaming out to Don, "Not my Chaddie! Not my Chaddie!" I pounded on his big strong chest in a primal cry like a lioness calling out for her cub taken by the jackals.

Breathe, just breathe.

We stood there not knowing what to do. Suddenly, it occurred to me that I needed to call Jerry, Chad's older brother. I didn't want to risk him finding out this horrific thing from a TV newscaster or social media.

Jerry had been Chad's protector since birth. There was a ten-year difference in their ages, and Jerry loved Chad so.

Jerry and Chad were as different as night and day. Jerry liked to fight things out, and Chad liked to talk things out. Chad adored and always looked up to his big brother. Jerry would have whooped Chad good if he'd needed it, but he would have also gone to battle for Chad if he had seen him in trouble. They were half-blooded brothers, but that blood was definitely thicker than water. Their bond was strong.

I called Jerry and simply told him that Chad was gone.

Through his tears, Jerry told me, "Oh, no! Mama!" He told me he had to come to be with us, and I could barely understand anything he was saying. This big, strong cowboy son of mine was sobbing so uncontrollably that his words were impossible to decipher.

About that time, Chad's wife, who had been sitting silently, jumped up and declared that she must get to their daughter, our precious granddaughter. Just as quickly, her parents and a few of her friends followed her out the front door of the Kyles' home.

We didn't know what to do either, so we jumped into action and followed right behind. In the meantime, I told Jerry to meet us at Chad's in-laws' home. Still feeling lost and alone, I called our pastor and a dear friend from church. They also agreed to meet us there.

It was sometime just after 11:00 p.m., and we trekked these dark winding roads in blind faith just following the other cars.

It was a foretelling of the road ahead of us.

Dark.

Twisting.

Turning.

No way to see up ahead.

Lonely and scary.

Dark.

Dark.

Soon we arrived at the home where Chad's little family was. The numbness had fully engulfed me, and Don and I stood there detached from the scene. At some point, I looked across the room and saw our son, Jerry. As if the Red Sea had parted open for us, we rushed to one another and fell into each others' arms. There were no words, only hugging and holding and sobbing. For that brief moment, we were safe and together with the only ones who could truly understand the depth of the moment. Instantly we were forever changed, clinging to the ones we knew and loved with the biggest hole blown through all our hearts.

Our pastor, Drew Erickson, and my friend, Angie, joined us. It was there that we formed a tiny protective circle of love, support, and prayer. Finally, sometime in the 1:00 a.m. hour, I kissed my beautiful little granddaughter goodnight. Her words shattered my already breaking heart as she asked me, "Memaw, is this a nightmare?"

I was inconsolable and although I longed to hold her and never let go, I left her there, just praying she would feel safe and protected amidst the sadness that was thick in the night air. There were counselors, ministers, family, and friends surrounding them also. My heart cried out to the Lord in silent screams only he could hear, asking him to hold her close through the night.

The long drive back to our house was like a movie reel playing and rewinding and playing over and over. There were a thousand unknowns and questions.

It was nearly 2:00 a.m. Don and I walked into our home and wandered around aimlessly as if we were in some unknown place looking for something to do, somewhere to be, someone to tell us how to proceed. We were exhausted beyond belief, all the way down to our souls.

Five hours earlier we had been getting ready for bed… *before the phone call that changed the world.*

Twelve hours earlier I had contact with my Chad. He was alive and well. Now, he was gone, forever.

Don had fallen asleep, and I paced and thought, trying to re-analyze what had happened.

Why?

Why?

Why?

I didn't want to deal with this. I didn't want this to be real. All I wanted was to be with my Chad.

Where are you, Baby? What's happened to you?

How has this beautiful day ended in this horror?

I have experienced losses of many kinds, but I had never hurt so deeply in my life as I did in those wee hours of February 3, 2013. For the first time I truly understood what it meant for someone to die of a broken heart.

Chapter 2

One Foot in Front of the Other

In those hours before daylight, I watched the news stations replaying the same clips that Jerry and Colten had been seeing the night before. Over and over they repeated the same thing, that Chris Kyle, the American Sniper, and another person had been murdered. The other person did not have a name yet, and so began my additional hurt. *My son* was murdered and yet he was "the other person."

"He's my baby! He's Chad Littlefield!" I screamed inside, feeling insult on top of injury.

I went to my computer and sat down to check Facebook. It was abuzz with the news of Chris Kyle's murder also, and I simply couldn't take it anymore. I didn't know a lot about how to navigate my own way around on Facebook, but I knew enough to take out some of my pent-up emotion. I posted that my son had been murdered alongside Chris Kyle. My son had a name!

Sleepless and frustrated, I decided that at 6 a.m. I would begin the task of tackling the long list of family members who needed to be contacted. For as long as I can remember, I have been a person who just does what must be done, so I put on my big girl pants and started making phone calls. Don was awake by this time, so he did the same, making calls to the Littlefield side of the family.

My first call was to my brother, who had traveled from Texas to Mississippi to tend to his own adult son who had been burned in a fire only two weeks earlier.

He made quick plans to return to us since his son was stable and improving.

Next, I called my three sisters. Finally, I called my cousin who lived about seventy-five miles from my eighty-eight-year-old mother. I thought perhaps she might have a phone number for a local clergy member in my mother's little Oklahoma town. I knew I could not emotionally handle being the one to tell her that her grandson had been murdered. My mother's identical twin sister lived right next door, but because of her age and health, I didn't believe she could be much of a practical help to Mother.

All I knew was that I had to get word to her quickly and personally before she heard it on TV in what had rampantly become a nation-wide news event.

Graciously, my cousin offered to go to Mother immediately, so she and her husband would be the ones to tell Mother face to face. My cousin assured me they would stay with my mother for comfort and then have her call me when she could. This one single act of kindness was a gift to my aching heart and one that I will never ever forget.

A few hours later, I did receive that call from my mom. We didn't exchange many words, but we cried together and we both needed that. She expressed her desire to come to me, but we both knew that was impossible at the moment because I was the person who normally picked her up and brought her down to Texas for visits with the family, and I was in no shape to do that.

By the time she and I finished, the phones started ringing and folks we had not seen in years were knocking on our front door. Apparently, the word was out. We got a call from our daughter-in-law, so we went back to where she and her family were and waited. About 6 p.m. we received word that Chris and Chad's bodies were being transported from the Dallas medical examiner to the funeral home in Midlothian. This was sooner than expected.

Don and I, Jerry and his wife, Teresa, and a few others gathered under the canopy at the funeral home and waited for this solemn private procession. We watched as two squad cars followed by two hearses and then two more police vehicles approached and turned in one by one under the canopy.

I looked over and observed a police officer standing just next to the flagpole where an American flag and a Texas flag were flying and in the middle of this dark event, I felt a great deal of pride and patriotism.

I didn't know which vehicle held Chad's body. I desperately wanted to rush to Chad, but I knew better. I was especially guarded about what images I allowed into my mind because I knew they would be stored in my brain's database forever.

Chad passed by so close and yet he wasn't there at all.

No one spoke. We stood there unified in silence as the tears poured down our cheeks. Our voices were silenced but the tears thundered down freely.

And just like that, the funeral director closed the doors into the funeral home where they had taken my Chaddie. We stood silently and knew it was time to go.

I shook hands with the police officers, thanking them each for escorting my son to this place. Then we sorrowfully got into our cars and headed home.

When we arrived home that evening we discovered that the front door was covered with handwritten expressions of love and sympathy. It looked like a Post-it Note factory dotted with color and stuck on with love. So many folks had come by to love and comfort us, and I was so sad that we missed them.

I continued to march forward as a good little soldier while on the inside I was still holding on to the hope that I might be shaken or pinched to discover that this really was all just a horrible dream.

Instead, the bad dream continued.

So did I.

Chapter 3

Not Alone

The next few days were filled with activity all around us. Family, friends, and long-lost acquaintances popping in here and there to show us their love and support. There was emotional overload and, simultaneously, information deficit. As things progressed, we became increasingly aware of the magnitude of this story into which our son's shocking death had been inextricably woven. We found out that while Chad's body was still lying in the dirt for hours, the person responsible had already been apprehended and moved into police custody. At the time of the shooting, Chad's wallet and cell phone were both in Chris's truck, so when authorities arrived, they had no way to quickly and immediately identify *the other man* because the perpetrator had fled the scene in Chris' truck. There was one determining factor that allowed Chad to be positively identified. It was his tattoo. He had a tattoo of Jesus on his shoulder.

When Chad and Jerry were growing up, we had a rule in our household that no son of ours would get his ear pierced or get a tattoo. Call us old fashioned, but that was just one of those things we didn't want them to do. I even went so far as to say that if they ever did they would be kicked out of our house.

So naturally as soon as Jerry moved away to college, he got his ear pierced. I hated it, but at that age, I didn't think there was much for me to do about it except grin and bear it. He already knew how we felt.

One weekend Don and I had gone to Oklahoma to take care of some things with my mother. While the cats were away, the mouse did play. Chad snuck off and got a tattoo on his ankle, strategically placing it so he could cover it with a sock. He was apparently in some pain after getting it and called Jerry to come over and help him. When Jerry saw what Chad had done, he told him to go ahead and pack his bags because when Mama heard about this, he would be kicked out! Chad managed to keep that tattoo covered somehow until just before graduation. He was almost out the door of our house on his way to college by then, so I threw my hands up in surrender and decided there were bigger battles to fight than that one.

As fate would have it, Chad later got another tattoo. He had an image of Jesus Christ on his shoulder. He had accepted Christ as his savior when he was eleven and had grown into a true man of faith. He wavered now and again from his faith, but his faith never wavered from him. He was never one for an abundance of words and since they say a picture is worth a thousand words, he let his tattoo make a statement for him. He wasn't ashamed of his faith; he just was never one to get in your face with it.

He identified his life by his savior, Jesus, and it turns out that he was identified in death by him as well. That tattoo on his shoulder had been his quiet statement to the world in his life and it was his final identifying statement to the world in his death, too.

I like to imagine Jesus when he welcomed Chad into heaven saying, "Well done, my good and faithful servant. Well done."

So, while my son had laid there in a pool of his own blood, the man whom Chris and Chad had generously taken out that day to try to build up had selfishly and ruthlessly shot them down. Thoughts like this haunted me. Amidst the hustle and bustle of caring people wrapping their arms around me, around Don and Jerry, and around our family, images of things I had not even seen flashed intrusively into my mind's eye.

I was thankful in some ways for the many distractions that helped to occupy my racing mind.

As the news story grew, it became obvious that we needed to make some kind of statement to the press. Our home phone rang non-stop with people from newspapers and TV stations perpetually requesting information and interviews. I suddenly understood why they are called *the press* because they were aggressive in their pursuit of any little morsel they could grab to build a story. The pressure we were feeling from their relentless phone calls and messages was inescapable.

On Tuesday evening, only about seventy-two hours after this ordeal had begun, we asked our pastor, Drew Erickson, to speak to the media on our behalf. We weren't prepared to be eloquent or even just to speak publicly, so he went before the cameras for us.

We had lived a quiet, private life that didn't seem to draw any special attention for years and years. In an instant, our privacy was gone. Strangely, it wasn't because of anything we had done, good or bad. It was because a madman had unleashed his terror upon our little world.

So much frenzy had come along with all of this. Things you would never think about had to be thought of. With the news reporting our coming and goings, a DeSoto police officer had to be placed in front of our house for our protection.

There was a city ordinance that stated that it was unlawful to block a mailbox by parking in front of it. There was no way to control the number of vehicles or their choice of parking and a blocked mailbox meant that mail would not be delivered to that address. We knew that pension checks arrived at the beginning of the month and worried that some of our very gracious neighbors might suffer because of the traffic surrounding us during this time.

A good friend of ours who was a member of the Patriot Guard Riders, Jerry Hall, asked if he could help us in some way. His timing was perfect, and his offer was sincere, so we took him up on it. He really lifted a burden from my mind by taking on the task of coordinating with the DeSoto Police Department as well as the postmaster.

Special arrangements were made with the postmaster, and he agreed to have our mail carrier hand deliver to the boxes on our street temporarily so that no one would be inconvenienced, except our mail carrier!

These details sound trivial, but they plagued my thoughts. So many little everyday things to think about, and my mind would carry that burden were it not for the kindness of others. More people than we could count were lending helping hands in our time of need.

We learned later that the men in Chad's neighborhood gathered in the street in front of his house. They stood in the cold night, in silence at first, but then sharing memories of funny things Chad had done... things Chad had said... about the many times they had all played basketball together. They stood together, grieving for their friend, grieving for the other man down.

Much to my surprise, a cousin who lived in Iowa drove down to Oklahoma, picked up my mother, and brought her to us so that she could be present to attend the funeral of her murdered grandson. It meant so much to us to be loved in such a variety of tangible ways.

The next twenty-four hours leading up to the visitation were a blur. Physically exhausted and emotionally void, we pressed on. Even though the interactions with people were incredibly taxing, they provided us with such a sense of awareness that we were not alone.

I felt completely alone with this in many ways, but no matter how I felt, I knew I was not alone.

"Be strong and take heart, all you who hope in the Lord."

— Psalm 31:24

Chapter 4

In the Wake of It All

Thursday Evening, February 7, 2013

How does a person choose what to wear to their own son's funeral visitation? With all of the special events in life, this was one I had never considered.

The weather was cool, and I expected to be on my feet, face-to-face with lots of people, so I wanted to look respectable and still be comfortable enough for the task ahead.

The visitation was scheduled to begin at 6 p.m. and end by 8 p.m. However, because these were small town folks who take care of each other and there was lots of media attention, people were drawn out to this visitation like we had never seen. There was a crowd by 5 p.m. and it grew to be a line that wrapped down the road over two blocks away. There were hundreds and hundreds of people standing in the street.

When we arrived, the weather was warm. As the evening progressed we were amazed to realize that a cold front had moved through, and people were standing outside completely underdressed and enduring the elements. When person after person greeted me and I felt their icy cold skin against mine, I was overwhelmed by the sacrifice so many were making just to show their respects.

That included family, church family, friends, military veterans, acquaintances, North Texas Patriot Guard Riders, off duty police officers, and so many more... all there for my Chad, and for us.

Despite of the fact that Chad never served in the military, he had always loved and respected those who did. That's what had drawn him to go with Chris to the range that Saturday.

Here we were only five days later, standing in a funeral home with our son's body lying in a casket. There were two Navy SEALs who stood as Honor Guards next to Chad's casket. Had Chad known it, he would have never allowed them to honor him, but as his mother, I was pleased and proud to see them standing over him.

The Patriot Guard Riders had committed themselves to us and our family, using their motorcycles to form a majestic wall of waving flags. The PGR are a group of volunteer motorcyclists riders who escort military and veterans to their final resting place. They lined the parking lot of the funeral home and their presence, impossible to miss, demonstrated their respect for someone important.

Chad was a simple person who delighted in making other people feel important. He had seen his fair share of mischief and made plenty of mistakes. He had also done a lot of really caring things. He was as human as any of us. No, Chad wasn't perfect, but he was loved, and he was important to us.

Four and a half hours later, around 9:30 p.m., we greeted the last of those paying their respects and wearily loaded up to head back home for another short night that would lead to another long hard day on Friday, the day of Chad's funeral.

As I reflected on this, I was overwhelmed by the volume of people who came out that evening to be with us. There were somewhere upwards of 1,500 to 2,000 people who showed up that night in a town of only about 15,000. That should have foretold to us what the next day would be like. My simple upbringing down in the Rio Grande Valley back in the fifties and sixties had not prepared me for the fanfare and attention attached to this very personal and intimate, yet public event. I was sharing the loss of my baby boy with the world around me and there were moments I simply didn't know if I could endure.

Sometimes all I could say, or think was, "I CAN'T do this! I can't DO this! I can't do THIS!" Looking back, I can see that all the while when I was saying those words, I WAS doing it. That was part of the mystery of just making it through.

And I did.

I'm still standing.

Chapter 5

Funeral Daze

Friday, February 8, 2013

Friday morning came, the day of Chad's funeral.

I heard the sound of heavy machinery outside my front door and opened it to find a man on a bulldozer coming down our street. I walked out in disbelief and asked him what he was doing, and he told me that he was going to be tearing up the road so they could repair it.

To which I impulsively replied, "Oh no you're not!"

What in the world?

Dear God, not today.

There are so many people who will be trying to come to our house.

What are we going to do?

After a brief exchange with the man on the bulldozer, he made a phone call to the city and, before I knew it, the whole project had been postponed. I knew this had to be a huge inconvenience to the man in charge because our street was on his punch-list and he needed to get the work completed in order to get paid for the job. That man went out of his way to rectify the situation at his own loss in order to show us kindness and respect during our time of grief.

Instead of reeling against the inconvenience, his own wife showed up and she swept the sidewalks to free them of the debris that had been created by the little bit of work that was started that morning so that all of our family and friends would be able to walk to and from their vehicles and our home without any obstacles. I couldn't believe the thoughtfulness.

There was so much surrounding this moment that it still didn't seem real in so many ways. I was there, but I wasn't there. It was happening, but it wasn't happening. Only, it was happening.

We loaded up and headed to the funeral home. As they wheeled Chad's casket to the hearse, I ached to reach out to him, to hold him, to have a private moment with my baby boy once more, but that didn't happen. And I marched on.

More than 200 Patriot Guard Riders lined up to escort Chad's body to the funeral. Midlothian Parkway was decorated up and down both sides of the road with beautifully flagged motorcycles and their tough, but tender riders. This gesture was an exception to the rule considering Chad never served in the military.

The Baptist Church in Midlothian had a sanctuary with a seating capacity of 1,000. In addition, they had also prepared some overflow spaces with audio/video feeds, anticipating more than 1,000 possible attendees. As it turned out, every space was filled to overflowing and people also stood lining the walls all around.

Once again, the outpouring of support was beyond measure.

In only three more days, we would have been celebrating Chad's thirty-sixth birthday, but instead, we mourned his departure from us in this life.

The Littlefield family and all its extended parts took up rows upon rows of seats. We sat in solidarity and sadness, yet we also had hope of seeing Chad again one day, not soon enough, but the next time we did we would never have to be apart again. That was the hope that held us together even in that worst moment.

I don't remember a lot of the details of the service, but I know Chad was honored, and we were loved. One of Chad's buddies wrote a poem and read it during the service that day:

Chad Littlefield

On February 11, 1977, God sent us a gift straight from Heaven.
We gather here today to celebrate your life,
Freed from this world of struggle and strife.
As the tears stream down my face,
I know God has taken you to a better place.

Why, I don't know, but it's not my choice,
I wish just one last time I could hear your voice.
Just remember as you walk the street of gold,
Our friendship will never grow old.
For our time on earth is pulled apart,
You will never be far from my heart.
Thanks for the memories, the good and the bad,
You truly were the best friend I ever had.
Kind, caring, compassionate and full of love,
A true miracle sent from above.
As for your family,
I extend my wing and ask, "Come fly with me."
Under my wing carefully guarded they shall stay,
I will help comfort and love them in every way.
You were such a good friend, this is the least I could do,
I pray to God to be as good as you.

— *Chet Kelley*

As the funeral ceremony came to its end, Chad's pallbearers carried his casket out to the hearse. Chad's wife and baby girl, who was seven at the time, followed behind, and I watched it all, again in disbelief, and somewhat disconnected. There was such a finality to everything. It was almost unbearable.

Grief is like a Shipwreck

Grief will come in waves. At first it is 100' waves.
When the ship is wrecked, you are drowning,
With wreckage all around you.
Everything floating around you reminds you of the beauty
and the magnificence of what was and is no more.
All you can do is hang on to anything that floats
while the 100' waves keep coming...
(continued)

This small anonymous article brought comfort to my heart when I didn't have the words to explain the feeling of grief, especially in moments like these.

Our 200-bike PGR escort rode with us out to the tiny country cemetery where Chad was to be laid to rest. Folks lined the roadside with their children waving the American flag as we passed. The graveside ceremony was a much smaller crowd. We gathered round the 2½-foot by 8-foot hole in the ground saying our final goodbyes.

We would never be so close to Chad's physical body again.

One Week Earlier, Friday, February 1, 2013

Chad worked near our house and it was not unusual for him to pay us a visit. That day (the day before the shooting) he came in and had lunch with Don and me. What was unusual was that he stayed for more than three hours just talking about his life, his family, and how things were going.

He told us how he was doing in his relationship with God and how his little girl was thriving at the new church they were visiting. He joked that he needed to brush up in his Bible stories because she was getting ahead of him!

In that last face-to-face conversation we had with Chad, he had said (in reference to his buddy, Chris Kyle), "I would take a bullet for him." Of course, he didn't know what was ahead, but even then, when he said that, I had quickly told him to stop talking like that because I didn't want to hear it.

"Greater love has no one than this: to lay down one's life for one's friends."
— John 15:13

He sat on our couch and said, "God has been so good to us it's scary!"

Don and I walked him outside, he hugged and kissed us goodbye and walked down the sidewalk to his truck, sat a package down inside the truck and for some unknown reason, he turned around, walked back up the sidewalk, hugged and kissed Don again, kissed me on the forehead, said, "I love you," once more, walked back to his truck and drove away.

In the next couple of days, I replayed that final encounter we had with Chad over and over. It is the most bittersweet memory I could have ever asked for.

When I focus on Chad's life being taken by his murderer, I can't bear it.

When I focus on knowing he willingly went that day for a troubled Marine and for Chris, well... that was Chad's heart and I can reflect on that joyfully anytime.

We never saw Chad alive again.

His stay was much longer than I had expected, and my mind had raced to all the things I neglected to do during those extra few hours of his visit. Little did I know, I would cherish those moments the rest of my life. Little did I know that there would never be another lunch together, no more chats on the couch, no more Chad "interruptions" to my never-ending list of to-dos.

To Feel Your Kiss

I watched you walk that morning,
As I had a thousand times,
But then stopped and turned around,
Your smiling eyes met mine.

One more kiss before you leave;
I wonder if you knew,
I'd need that kiss to cherish,
Each time I thought of you.

Now as I wake each morning,
My thoughts are always there,
Your gentle kiss upon my cheek,
I smell your precious hair

I cannot live without you,
And so, I've found a way,
To take you everywhere I go,
This simple prayer I say,

"Lord Jesus, far above me,
Please show me the way,
To know my Chad is with You,
To help me through this day."

"You can find him through Me,"
Is the message I receive
"Join us in the Spirit."
A gift of grace if we believe.

And so, I'll take you with me,
Everywhere I go.
Through me the sun will warm you,
Will share the glistening of the snow.

You will smell your daughter's hair,
Each time I hold her near,
Through our connected spirits,
You'll have all that's dear.

No one can take it from us,
This secret that we share.
It's not for the faint-hearted
The leap of faith we dare.

This morning I can sense you.
I see your loving smile.
I know we'll be together
In just a little while.

Until that day arises,
My heart our spirits share,
Each time I feel your tender kiss,
I'll know that you are there.

I bow my head and ask my God,
For the son I'll always miss.
He softly wraps me in His arms,
Once again, I feel your kiss.

— LeAnne Roberts, friend

His funeral was over and a full week without him in our lives had come and gone. After we made it through the maze of unknowns following his sudden death, I wanted nothing more than to close the door, turn out the lights, crawl into my big bed, pull the covers over my head, and just stop this crazy world from spinning. I wanted off the horrible terrifying ride. I wanted to wake up and discover the bad dream was over, but in reality, it was just getting started.

I told Don I could not think of anything wrong that Chad had done, and Don said, "Let me refresh your memory. Remember when he was maybe eight or nine years old, and you and Jerry stepped out onto the back porch? In sync, you and Jerry spotted smoke rising from the other side of our fence. The sound of a child's voice was cursing like a sailor and you quickly marched out the gate to investigate. Do you remember saying, 'I don't care who that kid is, but I know he won't be playing with **my** kid anytime soon!' As you rounded the corner, you found **that kid** to be Chad. He and a neighbor friend had built a fire on the concrete and as it grew they saw it was beginning to lick the motor of our neighbor's boat. Had another minute or two gone by, the gas tank of that motor would have probably exploded.

"You and Jerry managed to put out the fire under the boat. You promptly took Chad inside and lit a new fire underneath his butt. You wanted to make sure he remembered just how much fun it was to play with fire."

"Okay, okay," I said to Don, "Chad wasn't perfect."

Chapter 6

Mountains, Valleys and Shadows

Monday, February 11, 2013 was a big day. This was the day of Chris Kyle's funeral. It was also the day of Chad's thirty-sixth birthday. A day which would have otherwise been a family celebration had it not become a national day of mourning.

In some ways, attending Chris' funeral service was good for us. It gave us somewhere to be and something to do, and it was another thread which wove our unfolding heartache together with the Kyle family.

The service was larger than life. I was glad Chad's service had come first. I had needed that. It had given me the opportunity to say goodbye to Chad first and to attend Chris' funeral in support of the Kyles.

I loved Chris Kyle and his family, and my heart broke for them that they had to know this tragedy at all. After years of military service in the worst parts of the world, Chris had returned home to safety and to family. He had been working so hard to try and find a new normal, to make purpose out of his life. And all for what? So, one of his own fellow military veterans could gun him down in the middle of an unselfish act of kindness?

Chris and Chad had met on the soccer fields while their girls played together. Their personalities just clicked, and they became fast friends. Both guys like working out and they decided to start working out together early in the mornings in Chris' garage.

They were just two ordinary guys hanging out, dealing with life and stress, and figuring their way out alongside each other. Their 5:00 a.m. workouts sometimes didn't include much talk at all, just grunts and barbells and male bonding.

Chad's relaxed nature and good listening skills made him easy to open up to and somewhere along the way, their friendship had met a need for Chris as well as it had for Chad.

Chris started taking Chad along with him when he went to some big events that helped to raise money for veterans. Chad was a perfect fit for this because he was happy doing things behind the scenes, just being helpful. He loved veterans and he had experience interacting with them. He had set up lots of exercise and medical equipment for patients through his job.

At one of these events, Chad was introduced to a man who had substantial status, and the man seemed to know Chad immediately after hearing his name. Chad tried to correct him, thinking he had confused him with someone else who had served in the military.

The man said to him, "You're the one who brought Chris out of his darkest hours."

All along, Chad had known the value of working out to stay in shape and Chris had known the value of working out for his own mental health. They made the perfect pair. While they bench pressed and deadlifted, they were lifting each other's spirits as well. All they knew or cared about was that what they had worked for them and they both enjoyed it more when they were together. Their friendship had nothing to do with fame or spotlights. In fact, they did most of their friendship quietly and away from the outside world and that suited them both just fine.

I couldn't imagine all that the Kyles (his wife, his children, his parents, his brother) were going through, and they were doing it under a much bigger, brighter spotlight than we were. And I didn't envy that at all.

As Chris' funeral played out, I was blessed so deeply when Taya made mention of Chad. She said that he had an "easy smile" and that Chad had "blessed Chris with a friend that was the one that Chris needed more than anything."

Taya showed such grace and dignity both on and off the stage. The same intentional kindness she showed toward us publicly was what we received from her in the private moments also.

We watched her in amazement as she gathered herself and her two young children to square off with this harrowing, unwelcomed event.

There were brief seconds where I felt swallowed up in the bigness of the thing. Here I was, a tiny little dot in the sea of faces who had shown up to pay their respects to Chris Kyle.

In any other setting, I would have been thrilled to be close enough to see the countless famous faces I saw that day: Randy Travis, Neal McCoy, Randy White, Troy Aikman, Jerry Jones, and Sarah Palin. But the one that will stay with me forever was Todd Palin.

Todd hugged me warmly and said to me, "We will get through this."

I quickly replied, "Can you guarantee that?"

Todd looked at me squarely and compassionately and said, "We have no choice. We can crawl up and refuse to live or we can do what Chad would have wanted and go on with life."

Todd Palin was right. That is exactly what Chad would have wanted me to do and those words sunk deep into the chasm of my aching heart. I clung to them and drew strength from them in that moment.

"Have I not commanded you? Be strong and courageous. Do not be afraid and do not be dismayed, for the Lord your God is with you wherever you go."
— Joshua 1:9

Sometimes the well-placed words of a stranger were just what my heart needed in order to go on. Sometimes the timeless words of scripture became my sustenance, but whatever it was I needed, moment by moment, I was getting it, even when I didn't feel I was.

The afternoon funeral finally came to an end and we loaded up into the Midlothian Fire Marshall's SUV that was being driven for us. The whole experience had been quite an elaborate happening. There had been helicopters with sharpshooters, bomb-sniffing dogs, mirrors to check under all the vehicles, and Navy SEALs to buffer us all along the way. Once again, this was a foreign experience for this little ordinary Texas gal, and I was growing so weary.

Taya invited us to ride with the Kyle family the following day down to Austin for the procession to the Texas State Cemetery where Chris would be laid to rest. Although we were humbled to be included in this very personal aspect of their grief process, Don and I had simply grown too tired to withstand another fatiguing and emotional day. We declined their invitations and instead decided to finally try to start putting some pieces back together from this ongoing, ten-day long bombshell which had become our life. As the final hours of this day were drawing to an end, I had flashes of Chad's handsome face going through my mind. I had longings to just see him again. I wished to be singing '*Happy Birthday to you,*' once more, but instead I sat with the truth that all of this was our new forever reality. There was no going back, and I felt paralyzed, numb, and absolutely drained to empty.

Don and I watched some of the replays of Chris Kyle's funeral on the news before bed. Somehow watching it on TV, like the rest of the world, gave me another form of release and perspective. I was living it from the inside and watching it from the outside like the world around me was. I couldn't seem to shut it off in my mind. We felt compelled to watch this big event, even though we had attended it in person only hours earlier.

Over the next days, family and friends began to return to their own homes and lives in all their various places. As they did, I busied myself taking care of all things related to the aftermath of death in the family.

I wrote out thank you notes to dozens of people who had loved on us in a multitude of ways: meals delivered, house watching while we were away... the gestures are too many to name, but they were such powerful tangible expressions of love to us and our family.

I worked on getting my house back in order after the comings and goings of countless guests. I did as much as I could do to stay busy because that was my comfort zone. Despite my best efforts, I could not outrun the mounting grief that awaited me at every turn.

The comprehension of all this terrorizing reality was beginning to settle over me. As it began to sink in, I was overcome by an image.

The thought of this stayed with me all the time. There was a mountain and it was standing before me, enormous and immoveable. Each time I paused to even breathe, I could feel my face pressed right up to this giant of a mountain. No matter how hard I tried, I could not pull away from it. I could not see around it. I could not look past it. I could not even begin to imagine I could climb it.

But it was *my* mountain.

"I will lift up my eyes to the mountains – where does my help come from?
My help comes from the Lord, the maker of heaven and earth."

— *Psalm 121:1-2*

I tried my best to lean on God and what I know about his promises in the Bible, like his promise to "never leave you or forsake you" *(Deuteronomy 31:6, Hebrews 13:5)*, but some days I was just so weak.

Usually Don and I were kind of like we were on opposite ends of a seesaw. He would be up, and I would be down. I would be up, and he would be down. We gave our best efforts to try to lift each other up.

One day, Don and I both found ourselves in the depths. We didn't have the strength to lift our own heads, and we didn't have anything to try and uplift one another. We were in a downward spiral and it had a gravitational pull on us both.

In desperation, I cried out to God for help. I told him that he was asking too much. I told him, "I can't make it one more day! I don't want to make it one more day! What am I to do, Lord?"

There came a knock at our front door. I opened the door to find a chaplain from the DeSoto Police Department standing there. He stopped by to ask us if he might be able to come in and pray with us.

No matter how much I had believed in God before all of this happened, I was seriously in need of someone else whose faith could help to carry me. I was too weak to lift my own head and just at that moment, God had sent an angel to us. Don and I both firmly believed in God, but there were occasions when we needed someone *with skin on* to come be his arms to wrap around us and remind us that he was still there and that we could make it another day. That day, he came in the form of a police officer/chaplain.

"Even though I walk through the valley of the shadow of death,
I will fear no evil, For you are with me."

— *Psalm 23:4*

There was so much still ahead of us. When someone you know, and love, is murdered, you don't have the "luxury" of grieving in the same way as people do when they lose someone to death through sickness or even an accident. Murder meant that everything related to this death became overshadowed by news, public awareness, legal matters, police involvement, court appointed attorneys, and so much more. There was a sense in which something outside of our control was in charge of the timetable by which we processed our experience.

We were in for quite a bumpy ride, but preserving Chad's memory was our goal, so no matter how long or hard this road ahead, we were committed to seeing it through.

There is nothing I can do now about Chad being gone forever; his physical death is a reality, but it's also like a first death that is followed by a second. The second death is when people forget. We will never forget Chad, and we will always do everything we can to keep his memory alive. That is our mission... that is our dream.

It seems as if the human mind was designed to do things beyond even what we tell it to do. Dreams are one of those mysterious wonders that can take over our minds with or without our permission or cooperation. But sleep is needed in order to accomplish it.

The word "dream" is defined as "a series of thoughts images, emotions and/or sensations that occur in one's sleep."

Well, I had a dream. Just one.

In the time years since Chad's death in 2013, I have only dreamed about Chad once. It happened sometime after both guys' funerals when my mind and body must have taken a breath.

In my dream, I was seated in my usual spot in the den and looked up to see Chad walking through the back-patio doors. The house was filled with people and yet it seemed that no one but me saw or acknowledged Chad appearing. He stepped inside, shrugged his shoulders, and held out his hands with open palms, gesturing as if to say, "What in the world is going on in here?"

I jumped up and raced toward him, screaming, "Chad! Is that you? Is that you?" I reached out and put my hands on his shoulders, squeezing him hard. I rubbed his head, just as if he were my little boy and ran my hands over his arms, all the while continuing to shout, "Chad, is that you? Is that *really* you?!" I was like doubting Thomas, seeing for myself, touching his physical body with my own two hands.

While my one-on-one homecoming was taking place with just me and Chad, the rest of the room continued about their business, never noticing our interactions.

Together, Chad and I sat down on the couch and began to talk.

"Chad! We thought you were dead!" I told him.

As he and I continued to talk, we came to the conclusion that his death must have been a dream that everyone had dreamed and somehow everyone believed it was reality, when in fact, the reality was that he was very much alive, sitting right there with me talking. So, IN the dream, the dream was that we had dreamed his death, but he was really alive. When I awakened, once again, I discovered that the dream really was a dream and he was, in fact, gone. Dead.

Oh, how I wished that dream was true. I tried to return to that sleep and step back into that dream, to enjoy being in his physical presence once more. I would have given anything for that dream to be a reality, even if just for a moment. Touching him, sitting together, talking, face to face. That dream ended way too soon.

I have replayed it in my mind many times. I can close my eyes and see my big boy walking in through those patio doors again. After these years have now passed, I have grown to accept the reality of Chad's death a little more day by day, so I don't try to wish him back; however, I would settle for just the dream once again.

In my dream, for that brief window of time, that happened only in my mind, while I was sleeping, it was real. Chad was alive and I could touch him... hear him... see him.

Though I accept his death as reality now, I long to dream that dream just once more.

Chapter 7

April Showers Bring May Flowers?

There was something relieving about making it through the month of February and into the month of March. Just knowing that February 2013 was in our rearview mirror made the months ahead slightly more bearable, even though they were still daunting.

There were so many unknowns up ahead and so many unanswered questions. The details of Chad's death were still so patchy for us. Don, Jerry, and I really didn't know much more than the average person. We found out the few details we had by watching the news, and we were so anxious to have answers, even though we knew the answers would likely only create more questions.

Some unexpected family matters kept us busy during most of March. My mother's twin sister was growing ill and she had to be hospitalized near Oklahoma City, so we found ourselves making trips. First, we went to get Mom and bring her back to stay here with us, but it wasn't long before we had to return her to her sister's side. We were able to get there in time for them to have one final day together before my aunt passed away.

Suddenly, we had the added concern of how my eighty-eight-year-old mother was going to be after the loss of her beloved grandson and now her twin sister. The two ladies had lived next door to each other for years and were so close that my siblings and I had joked about having two moms and Don joked about having two mothers-in-law. It seems I may have gotten some of my toughness from her, because she handled things well, and we felt confident enough to leave her surrounded by cousins and other family as we headed back to Texas to try and deal with our own grief.

We wouldn't have chosen all of this, but it sure seemed to be part of a plan to give us someone and something to focus our mental and emotional energies on for a little while as a temporary distraction from the heartbreak of losing Chad.

In April, we received notification from Texas State Representative, Jim Pitts, that a formal resolution was going to be presented in Chad's honor.

Don, Jerry, and I were invited to Austin, Texas to attend meetings of both the House and the Senate. We were there when Senator Brian Birdwell read the resolution on the senate floor. Senator Birdwell presented each of us with his personal challenge coin.

We also were presented with the official Texas flag that had flown over the capitol on February 8, 2013, the day of Chad's funeral.

Every moment of this journey we were making was bittersweet. Sometimes almost entirely bitter and other times splashed with sweetness. Days like this filled our hearts with pride and joy, yet they were still sobering reminder that we would never see Chad again in this life. Sometimes the dark clouds hovered right over our heads and sometimes the rainbow peeked through, shining with the promises of hope amid this relentless darkness.

"When you pass through the waters, I will be with you; and when you pass through the rivers, they will not sweep over you."
— *Isaiah 43:2a(NIV)*

We were reminded that, at least for the moment, our Chad was being remembered. It touched our hearts, but there was quite a difference between the "Chad Littlefield" that the rest of the world acknowledged and the Chad Littlefield I had given birth to, raised, laughed with, loved, been loved by, and had proudly observed for nearly thirty-six years. I had watched his life unfolding before me, full of promise and sweet like the fragrance of a rose.

As I reflected on so many of those things I would miss about him, the days were passing. March became April, and April became May.

The first Mother's Day without Chad approached, and I longed to close my eyes and breathe in his scent just once more. The closest I could get to that was to go to my backyard garden and enjoy the fragrance of the Yellow Rose of

Texas that Chad had given to me a few years earlier.

Chad and I had exchanged yellow roses several times over the years. It had become our symbol of truce. If one of us needed to say, "I'm sorry" after we'd had a few words between us, we would use a yellow rose as our way to say it.

Once Chad had asked me what I wanted for Mother's Day, and I requested a yellow rose bush and asked him to plant it for me. He granted my wish. Sometime in the following years, I told him to look at all the crazy roses blooming on that bush. I said, "Chad, when your life is going well, that bush produces so many flowers, but when your life is not going so well, the little yellow buds are few."

Chad replied to me, "Yes, but Mom, if you had not watered it, fed it, and kept the weeds away from it, like you did for my life, neither of us would have produced." That was the Chad Littlefield that I knew and loved. As silly as it may sound, that rose bush was a bond between us. His words from that day are a memory I hold in my heart—so sweet, like the fragrance of the yellow rose.

Following Chad's murder that spring of 2013, my yellow rose bush didn't produce one single bud. Each day I checked for signs of life, and finally I cried to Don telling him my precious rose bush had died, too. It was like Chad was being erased, and I hated it!

One morning, only two days before that first Mother's Day without Chad, I walked by that bush and I was astonished to discover one single little yellow bud. Just one. One yellow rose for Mother's Day from my Chad. That was all I needed. I babied that little rose. I brought it inside; I gave it just the right amount of water and sunshine in hopes that I could keep it alive forever. As the petals fell from that rose one by one, it looked like teardrops falling. It was as if the rose was crying with me. Like Chad was saying, "I'm so sorry for your pain, Mom." My tears were plenty, but they were tears of both sadness and joy.

Even early on, I was beginning to see the little gifts from God that were hidden inside the most painful of things. Chad's little daughter was one of the pieces of Chad that we had left, and we loved her dearly. Only a few months after Chad's death, she chose to make Chad's faith her own. While attending Vacation Bible School, she prayed to receive Jesus as her savior and decided she would be baptized.

Well that baby girl called her Memaw and asked if her grandparents would be in town on a particular date because she wanted us to come see her be baptized. It was bitter-sweetness all over again. This precious monumental act of faith in her life was also a dismaying thought for me. If I were to go, I would have to see her be baptized only about ten feet from where Chad's casket had stood when I was last in that church.

Once again, I cried to Don telling him I couldn't do it. I just couldn't. My strong sturdy husband took me by the shoulders and said to me, "Yes, we are going. This means a lot to her and we will be there for her."

I put on my bravest face that day and we went to see my beloved Chad's baby girl be baptized. Unbeknownst to us, there was communion after her baptism. Her tender little heart was open but her young mind didn't fully understand what all of this meant. There was the bread, representing the body of Christ and the little cup of juice representing the blood of Christ.

I listened to Don as he whispered into her ear the meaning of each part. In my heart I could hear Chad say, "Thanks, Dad, for being with her on this important day and for standing in the gap for me."

I'm so very thankful for a strong loving husband who carried me when I needed it and for the grace I received that day, which enabled me to go. If I hadn't gone, I would have missed this chance God was giving me to hold on to Chad and at the same time, to let him go.

Making a beautiful new memory one day at a time has become like planting another yellow rose bush and getting to see the new little buds appear, one flower at a time. I was beginning to see that my Chad would always be with me no matter how dark the clouds, how long the night, or how deep the pain.

"Unless a grain of wheat is buried in the ground, dead to the world, it is never any more than a grain of wheat. But if it is buried, it sprouts and reproduces itself many times over. In the same way, anyone who holds onto life just as it is destroys that life. But if you let it go, reckless is your love, you'll have it forever, real and eternal."

— *John 12:24-25 (MSG)*

I have some special things that I will always treasure. They are pieces of Chad that I can never get more of and I can never replace. One of those special mementos is the last Mother's Day card I ever received from Chad, in May of 2012:

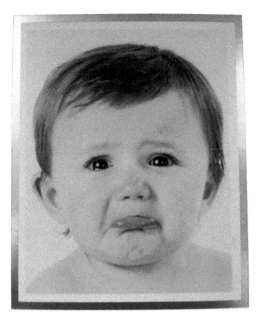

Mom,

I guess some things will never change, I will <u>always</u> be your <u>baby</u> and sometimes I still need my mother to take care of my owie's. I will always appreciate the time you take out of your life to listen to my problems, and give me guidance. Your opinion always matters and the advice you give is always appreciated. You have taught many important aspects of life, marriage, and most of all, how to be a great Daddy! The values you have instilled in your boys may continue on in our lives and our families. Thank you so very much for all you do for me, for my family, and especially my daughter. I hope I give back a portion of what you give me. Always keep you head up and your eyes on God, <u>So when I walk through the valley, or you walk through that valley we know where to take our problems.</u> I thank God every day that you are my mother and I hope you have a wonderful day!

Without moms,
Life would be
One big "owie!"
Happy Mother's Day

I'm proud of you and I respect you.

I am so blessed to have you in my life and I never take that for granted. Take care of your health so you can be around for many more of these special days, I love you with all my heart — Happy Mommie's Day.

Your baby boy — Chad

It is no small thing to see the hand of God at work. When I look back and re-read Chad's words, written in his own handwriting, saying to me, "so when I walk through that valley, or <u>you</u> walk through *that* valley we know where to take our problems," I have no choice but to honor the words he wrote.

I also can't help but acknowledge that he wrote in his own words, "*when* I walk through that valley, or *you* walk through that valley." I don't have any reason to believe that he knew he was going to die, but I can see the hand of God in his handwriting as I observe that for some unknown reason he underlined the word "you" as if it was meant for me to come back to later and see that God would use Chad's own words to comfort and guide me.

Don and I had taught him to turn to the Lord, and he was reminding me to do the same. Words he had written in his life were speaking to my soul in his death, and they were leading me back to life.

I was walking through the valley of the shadow of death... and God was with me, and so was Chad.

Chapter 8

Welcome to Erath County

About six months after Chad's death, we received information directing us to the Erath County District Attorney, Alan Nash. I was given a phone number, so I called to inquire for details. We craved anything that would inform us more about Chad's death and all the ongoing legal aspects surrounding it.

Chad's murder had taken place in Erath County at the Rough Creek Lodge and Resort's shooting range, near Glen Rose, Texas. The county seat was Stephenville, which was about a hundred miles away from us. This meant that Erath County was about to become our home away from home.

One thing I have learned is that everyone deals with loss differently, and Chad's wife opted not to be involved in the trial process, so Don and I became the active participants and communicators in all things trial related. I was ready to move forward in a surge of passion. Getting involved in the process gave me an outlet for my pent-up thoughts and feelings.

Even though much of my career life had been spent in law offices, I had never taken any criminal law courses and my legal assistant certification was in civil law, so I didn't know the proper protocol in a situation like this. The process surrounding Chad's murder was entirely different and entirely personal. I didn't know if I could call the D.A.'s office directly and expect to get answers, or if I would be viewed as a meddling mother, but we were so hungry for details that I decided to throw myself all in.

The staff of the Erath County D.A.'s office assured us that they would keep us informed about all of the upcoming proceedings. They promised to give us dates of every single hearing related to the trial. There was so much that had to take place before a trial date could even be set. They were faithful to their word and before long we got news that the decision had been made to try the defendant for both murders in one trial.

Chris and Chad had been murdered at the same location and in the same incident; therefore, it was considered one crime scene.

Everything about this experience was surreal. We were taking in information as fast as it was coming to us, yet somehow it was like we were learning to speak a foreign language.

Words like *murder, trial, defendant,* and *crime scene* were previously only spoken in our house if an episode of *Law and Order* or some such show was playing on TV. We were becoming fluent in this language, and we hated that we were learning it so well.

We were notified that one of those pretrial hearings had been set, and we locked it in our calendars. NOTHING could have kept us from attending. This was our chance to begin putting the pieces of this senseless puzzle together.

Another milestone in this sequence of events was that first date in August of 2013 when we would come face to face with the person who had taken the lives of Chris and Chad. It felt like progress because we were finally seeing some motion in the legal aspect, but it felt terrifying to think of being in the same space with this person who had single-handedly turned our world upside down and our hearts inside out.

Our emotions were all over the place, but after we got up in the early hours of the morning and dressed, Jerry and Teresa picked us up and chauffeured us the 100-mile drive to be certain we were there prior to the 9:00 a.m. court time. We truly had no idea of what to expect or how to act in a court of law, but we decided to walk in like we owned the place. We were fearful of our surroundings, but we went in and found that the courthouse was taking serious security measures:

No purses allowed.

All pockets emptied.

Shoes removed.

Belts off.

No cell phones.

This was real.

Once inside the courtroom, we watched a procession of prisoners in orange jumpsuits or black and white striped prison wear (apparently all the fashion in Erath County) as they were marched through with hands and feet in shackles. I felt like I was watching a scene from a movie, but we were *in* this movie and we couldn't get out!

Prisoners moved in front of the judge one after another until about 10:30 a.m. when the judge took a short break. All this time I could only wonder one thing... which one of them had killed Chad?

Which one of you did it?

Are you the one?

At the break, the district attorney and his staff came to us and introduced themselves. We had not communicated in person up to this point, so it meant a lot to us to put faces and names to this team of people who were working so hard on Chad's behalf.

Ever the realist, I thought they were going to ask us to leave, but instead they informed us that the defendant's case had been moved to 1:00 p.m., so they offered us a room to relax in until then. I should have taken my first hint then that this was how court cases go. Hurry up and wait. We were going to learn this lesson well over the course of all those upcoming months. The only thing predictable was that it would be unpredictable.

Around 1:30 p.m. we were ushered back into the courtroom to discover that all other cases and prisoners had been cleared out. There were no spectators except for us and a few members of the press.

The door to the left of the judge's bench opened, and we watched intently as the defendant entered the courtroom. I was surprised by his appearance. He was much heavier than in the photos they had shown of him on the news.

Do you have any idea the amount of pain you have caused us?

Do you know the Kyles are hurting just like we are?

Do you even care?

Are you sorry at all?

Don was seated on my left and Jerry on my right. I stared straight at the defendant as I gripped tightly to these two men I loved so much.

Suddenly, a flurry of thoughts and impulses surged through me. For a split second, an alternate scene played out in my mind's eye where I fiercely demanded him to tell me why he deserved to even walk this earth after he had taken *MY* baby's life! I envisioned myself reaching up and slapping his face, so hard and then again. I fantasized about beating him to a bloody pulp. I didn't just want "justice to be served."

I want to punish you!

I want you to experience the pain we're experiencing.

I want you to hurt like I hurt.

I want to hurt you like you hurt my Chad.

All of that happened in my mind in a few split seconds, then I was snapped back to reality only to realize that his attorney was asking the judge for more time to prepare their case. They were requesting a postponement to a later date.

We sat stunned and silent in this room lined with about fifteen armed law officers as the judge stood and then exited. The defendant was shuffled out quickly and taken back to the county jail.

Our day had begun eight or nine hours earlier and in fifteen minutes or less, it was over with nothing to show for it, or so it felt. We seemed to walk out with more questions than we had come in with, but we also believed our purpose that day had been served.

We were there to make certain that the world knew that *two* men had been murdered on February 2, 2013 and that *OUR SON* was dead. We wanted to make it impossible to ignore the fact that we cared, we were grief stricken, and we would not go away until we got answers.

We are Chad Littlefield's family.

He was shot and killed.

We want justice on Chad's behalf.

Even if I had to spend every ounce of life and breath left in me on this one thing, Chad Littlefield would not be overlooked or forgotten. My son was the other man down.

Erath County very easily could have become the most dreaded place in the world for us, however there were some priceless things that happened there, too. So instead of Chad's murder and trial being the only things we associated with this place, we were given some powerful expressions of love, kindness, and support.

As we were nearing that first Christmas, we were invited to attend and participate in the Erath County's annual Tree of Angels ceremony. The victim coordinator inquired if we were interested in partaking in this evening, which was designed to support families, friends, and survivors of violent crimes. Each participant was encouraged to bring an angel ornament in memory of his/her loved one, as acknowledgment of their encounter with some form of violent crime: murder, drunk driving, rape, domestic abuse, and much more.

Don and I talked about this invitation, and we decided that it sounded like something that might give us an outlet for our grief as we were blindly making our way through this uncharted territory.

We had an angel wing ornament made that we brought with us on the evening of the ceremony. We arrived at the courthouse and found that we were one family among many others grieving the loss of loved ones and the impact of a whole spectrum of violent crimes.

During the ceremony we lit a candle and had the meaningful privilege of adding Chad's ornament to the big beautiful tree which stood proudly inside the center of the courthouse throughout the holiday season.

It was an eerily awe-inspiring scene as we stood gathered among this band of fellow mourners and took in the magnitude and the unexplainable wave of healing this unique moment gave to us.

I can still see that horribly magnificent tree in my mind's eye, even now. It sparkled and shone with the countless angels that adorned it, each one representing someone just as loved and missed by another family as Chad was by us.

We had planned to do a number of things that Christmas of 2013 to memorialize Chad, but the Dallas area was stricken with several ice storms that immobilized us several times.

I am happy to say that attending that first Tree of Angels ceremony was so beneficial for us that we determined to create a similar experience for our church family, giving our friends an opportunity to honor their own loved ones. We've experienced and witnessed the substantial emotional impact of such a simple exercise.

Others may never fully understand the value of a tradition like the Tree of Angels ceremony, and that's okay because to understand it a person would have to go through a similar loss and that is a pain I wouldn't wish upon anyone.

Chad's ornament remains at the Erath County Courthouse where it is placed and displayed on that tree every year.

We have only missed one ceremony since 2013.

Chapter 9

The Wheels of Justice Turn Slowly...

Somehow, we made it through that first holiday season.

As January 2014 rolled around, we received a letter from the office of the District Attorney. Dates had been set for the case to move forward, finally.

- Pretrial, February 18, 2014
- Additional Pretrial, March 7, 2014
- Trial on Merits to begin May 5, 2014

After nearly a year in what felt like limbo (or better yet, purgatory) it was beginning to feel like we might get some traction. Every minute of every day we had been consciously aware of this cloud of darkness which had overshadowed our lives. Even acknowledging Chad's upcoming birthday became secondary to the February 18 date. We counted down all the way through January, keeping our focus on the anticipated relief that the pretrial proceedings would begin to bring to us.

On February 2, 2014, the first anniversary of Chris and Chad's murder, the public nature of our loss became virtually unbearable.

Some well-meaning but advantage-seeking business owners had their way. Burger joints were selling two-for-the-price-of-one burgers in honor of Chris Kyle. The news media was replaying clips of the "Chris Kyle murder" news footage from the year before.

Instead of us having an opportunity to quietly mourn and acknowledge the loss of our son, that day was like a circus.

In addition to feeling like Chad was perpetually overlooked, I also simultaneously felt deeply saddened for the Kyles, knowing that they, too, were trapped inside this nightmare. Our private loss had become public domain.

Infuriated beyond belief, I wanted to shake my fists and scream to the tops of my lungs, "Doesn't anyone care that our families are mourning? Did anyone ask the families how we felt about this?"

This day wasn't supposed to be a two-for-one burger day because what it really had been was a two-for-one murder day!

I felt betrayed to the very core of my being. I teetered back and forth between rage and heartbreak all day. I was physically nauseated that even a year later, my Chad was still a nameless victim, murdered alongside the American Sniper. And again, I hated myself for feeling anything but compassion for the Kyles. It wasn't that I wanted Chris to be minimized or ignored in any way, it was just so unbearably painful for my son to be overlooked. I needed to experience some form of public acknowledgment that he was just as important, just as valuable as Chris, even though he was not as known.

The Kyles had all expressed such kindness toward us and frustration on our behalf many times. It was the media that almost never gave Chad a name. It was beyond comprehension. The Kyles even acknowledged their frustration over the way Chad's name was repeatedly omitted, pointing the media back to the fact that Chris didn't die alone.

All of this was like a fire burning in my chest, and I would not be satisfied until I could see this trial through to the end. At the very least, those twelve jurors, the judge, the families—everyone in the courtroom—would all hear about the life and death of my son, Chad Hutson Littlefield.

On Tuesday, February 18, 2014, we arrived at the courthouse to be greeted by a woman who gave us her business card and introduced herself. She was from the Texas Attorney General's office. She explained that they would be assisting in the prosecution of this capital murder case.

In an instant, the magnitude of the case seemed to exponentially multiply, and, in some ways, that was both terrifying and relieving.

Unbeknownst to us, while we waited in the courtroom for the defendant to be brought in, a massive orchestration of security measures was underway to safely get him there.

A two-mile radius had been blocked off by law enforcement in every direction from the courthouse. Eight to ten officers were escorting him from the county jail all the way to the holding cell inside the courthouse. S.W.A.T. teams lined the roof tops of the square and three decoy vehicles had been part of the transport effort.

He seemed like a pretty important guy when we learned of all the measures that had been taken to ensure his safe arrival that day.

Who is he being protected from…us?

Seriously?

Maybe it's all a gesture to show just how seriously he is being handled?

At any rate, I could not accuse them of negligence when it came to their show of commitment to this process for getting the defendant to court so that he would face his due consequences.

Unlike the fruitless day in court in August of 2013, this hearing lasted several hours.

We were still grossly unprepared for things we would see and hear, even at this stage of the game. As the proceedings unfolded, we found ourselves agonizing through the defendant's confession which had been recorded on video by the police on the night of February 2, 2013.

As we watched and listened in shock, my mind raced back to that night when we had been called by Taya to come over. We had waited for hours in fear and anguish for the other man to be identified, hoping against hope that it wasn't Chad. While our suffering had been prolonged, this man… this beast… this savage had already sat down to confess his sins. The worst sting of all came when the Texas Ranger (on tape) asked him the name of the other man he had shot.

He simply replied, "I don't know."

In my heart I screamed out my son's name like the roar of a mighty lioness.

Chad Littlefield!

His name is Chad Littlefield, you idiot!

You killed him and you didn't even know his name?

YOU don't deserve this good treatment after what you've done!

Our hearts were shattered.

This man (and I use that word to identify his gender, not his character) had killed our son and he didn't even remember his name. I was beyond disgusted.

Chad didn't deserve this. My baby's spilled blood had been removed from the defendant's boot and was later identified through DNA testing. This was a gory detail, and it fractured my heart that day.

My baby's blood, poured out pointlessly in the dirt while this man drove away in Chris' truck, carrying Chad's only form of identification with him and leaving them both behind to die like wounded animals.

Maybe it was divine intervention to keep our hearts from rupturing, but the proceedings were brought to a halt due to technical difficulties. The video tape was breaking up, so the judge ordered a postponement until March 7 to allow time to get it in working order.

So once again, we went back home... to wait. We had just enough new information to relive and torment us until that date.

It seemed that this pause in the judicial process would also be another pause in our personal world as well. Life seemed to be something that everyone else was doing out there as we were trapped in this suspended alternate universe where we didn't dare make plans to go much of anywhere or do much of anything for fear that we might be unexpectedly called to the courtroom at any given moment.

No matter where we were or what we were doing, in the back of my mind there was always an escape plan being formulated that would get us back to Stephenville at the drop of a hat.

Even the most basic daily life tasks had some link in my mind back to Chad, back to this. I couldn't go to the store without a memory.

Once when Chris, Chad, their wives, and kids had gone on a trip to Port Aransas together, Chris got word about a soldier who had come back home. He was a double amputee and he was really struggling. He was on a base in San Antonio, so the guys decided to go spend the day with this young man while the wives and kids went to Sea World.

Chris thought it might be of some help to the soldier to read his book, but he didn't have one with him; he told Chad that they needed to swing by Walmart to buy a copy. Chad mocked Chris and told him there was no way Chris' book was for sale in Walmart.

The guys went in together, found the book section and, to Chad's surprise, there was a whole gigantic display designated specifically for the *American*

Sniper books. Chris quickly snatched one up, payed for it, and headed out.

Chad told Chris, "Wow, man! You really are famous."

They laughed it off and went on to spend the day with that struggling soldier, and that incident was the first time Chad saw Chris through any eyes except his own. Chad was the kind of guy who didn't care about fame, and Chris was the kind of guy who would walk into the store and discreetly pay for one of his own books just to bless a brother in need.

These were the kinds of memories that intrusively flooded my mind now even in the most ordinary of moments.

This perpetual suspended state of being was like hovering over a bed but trying to keep my body from imprinting on the sheets. Like never allowing myself to just collapse into it and feel supported. Technically, we were having moments to rest, but the important things weren't settled, so we never really rested. It was an ongoing restlessness.

Looking back, it does seem that God was giving us this time to work in and on our hearts, although we didn't see it or feel it at the time.

Don and I had decided early on that we had to be vigilant about the condition of our hearts. It would be so easy to let bitterness and anger creep in. Resentment, vengeance, and unforgiveness were always lurking at the doors of our hearts, threatening to overtake us and turn us into prisoners in our own lives.

We had seen plenty of people whose lives had been poisoned by bitterness and we were determined to become better instead. I had heard the saying "Staying bitter is like drinking poison and waiting on someone else to die." Regardless of the moment-by-moment struggle, we were committed to keep moving toward *better* and away from *bitter*. And we knew it would require the grace of God every step of the way.

Although every day between February 18 and March 7 seemed to move so slowly, our day back in court finally came. As we were approaching Stephenville once more, we decided to stop at a convenience store to refresh ourselves before driving on to the courthouse. While we were inside, the sounds of sirens blaring and coming from every direction nearly rattled things from their shelves. Police cars out on the highway were in sight and everyone inside the little convenience store was drawn to the windows to see what was happening.

About that time, one of the sales clerks spoke to me and said that all the activity was because they were transporting the prisoner who had killed the American Sniper and that the police would open the roads back up and we could all be on our way soon. This young woman, along with some of the other customers, proceeded to grumble about how having this guy around was inconveniencing everyone.

What a sobering and surreal moment.

As I listened to the chatter about "the prisoner" I was keenly aware of the fact that no one in the whole place had even a clue who we were. They were momentarily inconvenienced by his presence. In that instant, I knew just how different our lives would forever be because of this. That one little happenstance said it all.

For five minutes or less everyone else's world was inconvenienced, and they would soon be on their way back to whatever they had been doing before. That same set of sirens and police cars were transporting the man who had single-handedly robbed the world of Chris Kyle and Chad Littlefield, but the road ahead of us had a much more complicated set of potholes, detours, and challenges.

After the police opened the road again, we headed on to the Erath County Courthouse. Upon arrival, as before, there was a full security check. I knew that I would not be able to bring my purse into the courtroom, so I had tucked a few personal essentials into the pockets of my pants: a package of tissue, gum, and some mints. As we approached the deputy, I asked about emptying my pockets into the basket. I could tell he kind of recoiled as I reached into my pockets to drop the items in for clearance.

When my packet of gum appeared, the deputy said, "Lady, I thought you said your 'gun'!" When I realized he thought I was about to pull a gun out of my pocket and I was asking him if I needed to put it in the basket, I got a much-needed moment of private laughter. He and I smiled at each other, but on the inside, I was laughing hard as I pictured what could have happened in those few brief seconds of miscommunication. When the only piece I was packing was Dentyne!

We found our seats in the courtroom and waited with high hopes and feet planted firmly on the ground. Once again, those hopes were dashed.

According to the woman from the Texas Department of Public Safety Laboratories, there were hair samples extracted from Chris' truck, and the DNA process to confirm whose they were would require at least a six-month timeframe.

This one piece of information in one testimony was an instant guarantee that there was no chance of a trial beginning in May. In fact, it was determined that there would not even be a tentative trial date set again until the attorneys announced that they were ready with all the results of the requested lab tests.

It had been well over a year since Chris and Chad were murdered. If we learned nothing else from this painfully slow process of the justice system, we were bound to learn some patience and endurance.

Don, Jerry, and I still really had no idea of what had happened on that day, February 2, 2013, and it was clear we would have to wait a while before we might begin to get some of those questions answered.

Nothing, absolutely *nothing*, was more important in each of our lives than getting the answers to the never-ending list of unanswered mysteries surrounding the death of our precious son and brother, Chad Littlefield.

The Numbers Game

On one of our many trips back home from Stephenville, Don and I decided to find our way to the Rough Creek Lodge near Glen Rose, the location of Chris and Chad's murder. We set the GPS for Rough Creek Lodge and headed north on Highway 67. We saw a road sign for the lodge pointing us in the direction we should take. We looked up to see that we were turning onto County Road 2013.

2013... that was the year they were murdered. My mind immediately raced, wondering if the road had always been called "2013" or had it somehow been changed to be in sync with memorializing Chris and Chad?

Upon turning, we saw another sign that indicated that the Rough Creek Lodge was four miles ahead. Don, who is a numbers guy, said, "Look, they were murdered on the second day of the second month. Two and two. It's four miles ahead to the lodge. Two plus two equals four."

Its sounds a little silly, but we were grieving parents and our hearts and minds were constantly searching for pieces to the senseless puzzle, hoping to make something meaningful. Always searching. These coincidences with the name of the road and the distance to the lodge seemed to whisper to our souls in some way, telling us that God was in the details, reminding us that Chad mattered and that we mattered to him in the midst of our grief.

As we drove County Road 2013 to RCL, I couldn't help but picture Chris and Chad making that same drive. A drive from which they would never return.

It was a bone chilling experience we had that day, driving those four miles in solemn observance. When we reached the entrance to the lodge, we sat at the gate. We could go no further. What was beyond that gate was more than we could venture into at that moment. After Don and I had sat and took it in, we turned around and drove back up County Road 2013 to the highway, toward home. It felt wrong that Don and I were able to make that return drive home knowing that Chris and Chad were robbed of that same opportunity.

As we drove back, part of me wished we could somehow turn back the hands of time, like a rewind in a movie, where an alternate outcome is played. If only we could get back to Highway 67 and it would somehow push the reset button on the whole thing. I would have given anything to make that happen.

But no. Their memory would forever be paved into the curves of that hilly, windy county road. On the second day of the second month, four miles down County Road 2013 in the year 2013... they drove to their death with evil in the backseat. They chauffeured their own murderer right to the scene of the crime.

Chapter 10

To Plea or Not to Plea

In the weeks that followed I was invited by an acquaintance to come speak to a group of chaplains about our loss. The man who invited me was someone who I formerly attended church with, so even though I was scared, nervous, and questioning my ability as a speaker, I agreed to go. Having a room full of sympathetic people who would sit and listen to me talk about Chad and about the difficulties of life after a murder, well that was an offer I decided not to refuse. It was a good experience for me, and I think it was for them as well.

A week later, Don, Jerry, and I met with the district attorney, the assistant attorney general, and the court investigator. They requested a meeting to discuss some things with us, so they came to our home, which was both nerve wracking and comforting.

During our visit, the D.A. told us that he wanted us to weigh in on what we felt would be appropriate kind of sentence they should seek when it came time for the trial. What kind of justice would we like to have carried out?

There was no *justice* for Chad because *justice* would mean that he would never have been murdered, so we had to really think about this.

Having the power of life and death placed in our hands really didn't have the satisfaction one might expect in a situation like this. We really didn't want to be the ones to decide, and of course, we weren't the judge or jury, but no matter what, our words and decision would have an impact on a lot of lives, so we could not just base our decision on our feelings or desire to see an eye-for-an-eye action carried out.

Don and I agreed with each other, but Jerry was on another page.

Jerry was younger and more zealous.

We were older and more practical.

The idea of choosing the death penalty may have had some appeal to our sense of justice, but ultimately the thought of the defendant sitting on death row for twenty years while Don and I grew older or possibly even died prior to seeing him finally face his consequences was more than we were willing to endure. Jerry, on the other hand, was more driven by a desire to see him become an example to any others out there who might consider doing such evil against someone else in the future and his desire for the defendant to experience a consequence which paralleled his actions.

Ultimately, we decided life without parole would be a punishment we could live with, and we knew that finding a jury that would be willing to come to an agreement on the death penalty was also another potential obstacle to a death penalty conviction.

The fact remained, no matter what we decided, that Chad was still gone... for life, and that was *our* life sentence given to us by the man whose life was being placed in our hands.

A couple of years back I had made a promise to my mother, Chad's grandmother, that when she and her twin sister reached their ninetieth birthday I would throw them a big bash. Mom has always loved attention and I knew that ninety-year-old twins deserved to be celebrated!

Before they reached ninety, Mom's twin sister was hospitalized and passed away. Although her twin was gone, as their birthday was approaching, she made it clearly known that she was still looking forward to her birthday party.

Well, a promise is a promise. Despite how our grief for Chad was still very much overshadowing our daily lives, my sisters and I worked hard to put together a proper party for Geraldine "Jerri" Conlan, aka Party Girl.

Her birthday was in July and although we lived in Texas, we planned her party for June in her little hometown of Fletcher, Oklahoma. We sent out somewhere around one hundred invitations. We ordered cake, planned decorations, and rented out the Fletcher school cafeteria.

A week or two before her party, I received a call from the district attorney. He wanted to know how quickly we could drive back down to Stephenville.

Back in March, when we had all met together in our home, they had suggested a possible date of mid-June, telling us then that there might be a guilty plea offered by the defendant which would guarantee that he would forego trial by jury and, therefore, give him control over the unwanted possibility of a death sentence, ensuring life without parole instead. Little did we know three or four months earlier that this monumental family celebration would be interrupted by the ongoing process of the trial.

Every day of life was spent with Plan B always ready for another moment just like this. So, I handed off my part of the party planning to my sisters, and Don and I got back on the road to head home.

Making another drive to Stephenville, well, we could have done it with our eyes closed, or so it felt.

The Littlefields and the Kyles all had high hopes that the defendant would offer his plea, and we would finally draw in a collective sigh of relief as we saw an end in sight.

"Hope deferred makes the heart sick..."
— *Proverbs 13:12*

Our hearts were all growing weary, but our longings would have to wait to be fulfilled.

When we entered the courthouse that day, it was very different. The word that comes to mind is that it was eerie. There was no press. There was no security to speak of. I even asked where the security was, and I was told there was no need for it this time. It seemed the rules to this unknown game were perpetually changing. It was a new experience every single time.

Escorted into the courtroom, we were directed to sit on the right side of the room. The defendant's family would be seated on the left.

The tension in the room was palpable.

The overwhelming feeling in the air was anxiety... from all parties. At the left front of the room: the defendant, accompanied by three attorneys, came out, and they all took seats. Their backs were toward us.

To the right front: the district attorney and his prosecution team came out and were seated directly in front of us.

Only a center aisle divided us from each other.

The good guys on the right.

The bad guys on the left.

If only it were that simple.

This is awful!

Here we are, four mothers, all with broken hearts.

I can't stand this.

Here we are, me and Debbie both broken for our sons.

I know that the defendant's mom's heart is broken by her son's actions.

Taya lost her husband and the father of her little children.

Just like in the movies, we were instructed, "All rise, said the Honorable Judge Jason Cashon…"

Moments like these with all their gravity made the stresses of planning Mom's party seem like a piece of cake… no pun intended. If only I could have been back in Oklahoma instead. If only none of this was real.

As we were seated, I looked up at the D.A. to see him shaking his head. The prosecution team sat down, and I leaned over to Jerry and whispered, "What do you think that means? Why is he shaking his head?"

Jerry said, "Mama, it means he's NOT going to plead guilty."

My stomach dropped and the ever-present lump in my throat swelled again. Hope deferred, AGAIN.

With just a few short sentences, the judge made it official. The defendant had decided that he would take his chances. He wanted to go to trial.

The audacity of this man rattled me to the core.

You selfish, selfish man!

Isn't it enough that you took our sons…these husbands…these fathers?

Now you want to rule our lives for the next year while we hang in limbo.

It's not fair that YOU get to choose AGAIN how another chapter in all of our lives will play out!

Judge Cashon spoke directly to the defendant and his team of attorneys. He gave unmistakable directives explaining that from that moment forward, the State of Texas would move to trial. There would be a date set for trial. He would be tried before a jury of his peers.

We kept getting so close, or so we thought, and yet it was still so far away.

Everyone was again instructed to rise as the judge left the courtroom. The defendant was then escorted out immediately.

The courtroom erupted.

We were all so enraged, both the Littlefields and the Kyles.

It was good that he had the protection of the police escort because had we been able to get to him there is no telling what one of these Texas boys might have done.

We spent the next little while trying to calm each other down, but the fury was just irrepressible.

Once again, this man had turned our worlds upside down.

We had been told all along that it was entirely possible he would not plead guilty, but we had reasoned in our minds how crazy and stupid he would have to be to let it go to trial. I guess that's where our reasoning was flawed because he was crazy *and* stupid, or so it seemed to us.

It all seemed like another way for him to get attention, as if he strangely enjoyed being at the center of it all. He was like a rowdy child who would rather get in trouble than to go unnoticed.

After all, he had fattened up quite nicely since we had first seen him. He must have put on forty pounds. It appeared that jail life agreed with him, so I thought if jail life agreed with him, then he was going to love prison life!

The families were ushered to the district attorney's office, so we would all have a chance to simmer down. They wanted to decompress the air in the courtroom. Looking back, they might have been trying to protect us from ourselves.

Since the DNA evidence still had several months before it would be available (maybe September or October), we were informed that the trial date would not be set until then. We were also informed then that the State of Texas would be seeking the death penalty. That meant that if found guilty, he would be put to death by lethal injection.

We left there that day with a million more unanswered questions and hearts that were heavy for many reasons.

Our heavy hearts would have to be set aside once again. Due to the timing of the court proceedings, we had enough time to make it back to Oklahoma to attend Mom's ninetieth birthday party.

If emotions could have been switched on and off, it would have surely been a convenient time to flip that switch. We went from discussing the death penalty to a celebration of life. The feelings we faced were polar extremes and exhausting in every way.

We headed north again, stopping at home long enough to unpack, repack, and then make our way back to Fletcher in time for Mom's party.

Inside, the quiet of my heart I ached.

Physically ached, to just *stop*.

To grieve.

To rest.

To be weak and to find relief... but we just kept going.

All of this long drawn out agony and all because the defendant refused to just take the plea.

Chapter 11

Happy Holidays...

Our hot Texas summer dragged on and September finally rolled around. We knew there was a chance that we could hear about the DNA tests, but no, not a word.

We were invited again to speak to another group of chaplains toward the end of September. Just having something to look ahead to seemed to be helpful. October also came and went. No word.

We finally did receive word that 2014 would not be the year. With the holiday season approaching, there would be no attempt by the courts to schedule anything. We were told the holiday season was just too challenging to work around because people wanted to spend time with families.

Oh, really?

People want to spend time with their loved ones?

Yes, I understand.

So do I!

But no, MY loved one is gone.

Just knowing the holidays were on their way whether we liked it or not was a matter of white knuckling our way through. The idea of our family gatherings never including Chad and his family again made it so hard to face.

We had a standing invitation to attend the Annual Erath County Tree of

Angels ceremony, so we decided to go again. It had been so meaningful to us that first Christmas. We thought it might be another tiny step toward healing our hearts and we were right.

The very idea of seeing Chad's name and hanging his ornament brought a gentle soothing to my soul. As we gathered there again, in this same place that held such anguish for us each time we had come for pretrial court hearings, we were so comforted to be in the presence of the other families who also knew pain like we did. This private club, to which every family had unwillingly become a part, had a membership requirement which we all wished we didn't know. However, there was tremendous healing power in this shared space inhabited by all of us whose lives had been forever changed by violent crime.

It was like a sacred act, getting to place our commemorative ornaments on the tree of angels. My big tall husband hung our Chad's angel wings as high as he could reach so everyone who passed by could see.

My heart brimmed with love for this man and the rock he had been in my life for so many years. I knew it was breaking his heart to be there hanging that ornament on the tree again because he loved Chad so very much. Chad looked a lot like the younger version of Don that I had met way back in 1973.

Don was a tall, handsome usher who I spotted across the way one Sunday when six-year old Jerry and I attended the church of a pastor friend of mine from back home, who was in Dallas by then. The pastor wanted to introduce me to someone and to my very pleasant surprise, it was the well-dressed single usher, Don Littlefield.

A few weeks went by, and I contacted the pastor's wife to inquire about Sunday evening church services and she told me that the handsome Coach Littlefield had also recently inquired about me. This coach was Don Littlefield, the local junior high football coach. She passed along my phone number to him and, in less than thirty minutes, I got a phone call from him.

We went on our first date in March. We got engaged in October and on December 15, 1973, we were married.

So, this man had been my rock for many years by the time we lost our Chad. I had seen my rock be crushed through this traumatic event like no other hardship we had ever faced.

Don and I both shed cleansing tears for Chad. Our hearts hurt just knowing all these other people's hearts were hurting, too.

That very night, the D.A. gave us some encouraging news that the trial would very likely begin sometime in the near months of 2015. That night, it felt a little bit like maybe heaven was smiling down on us... just maybe.

Little did we know the beautiful gift the yuletide season still held for us.

"It's the most wonderful time of the year! With kids jingle-belling and everyone telling you, 'Be of good cheer!' It's the most wonderful time... of the year"?

Really? Everywhere we went, the sights and sounds of Christmas filled the air, while the sadness and dread filled our hearts.

Normally, the world never seemed more perfect and at peace than it did at Christmas time, yet our sadness weighed on us like a heavy blanket, so heavy it was cumbersome to bear. The holly jolly world around us just kept flurrying.

It never even paused to say, "I'm sorry you're hurting so badly while I sparkle and dance all around you."

I didn't have it in me to erect our Christmas tree. I imagined us going somewhere far, far away. Some place where Christmas didn't exist. I was missing Chad and his little family so much. I didn't know if or when I might see his baby girl again since they had relocated several hours away.

Each morning throughout December when I awakened, I wished for Christmas to be over, for all the gay happy meetings and holiday greetings to just be behind us.

We made it.

We made it through.

We woke up on December 26th and decided to make the seventeen-mile drive to the little cemetery where Chad was buried. The cold, drizzly, dreary day accurately reflected our hearts.

We had gone to retrieve the holiday wreath we had placed on his grave at the beginning of the month. We expected it was dead by then and would match the grass we had also tried so hard to breathe life into with no results.

As we approached the cemetery, I got out of the car to open the gate with cold mist hitting my face. Don entered, and I hopped back into the car. We pulled forward the short distance to the spot where Chad was buried.

We had always maintained small American and Texas flags, making it a little easier to spot each time we were there, but to our astonishment, someone had changed things. Don and I looked at each other speechless and amazed. We couldn't even recognize the grave site. We wondered if some other family had come in and somehow mistakenly been at the wrong site. We spotted the headstone with the word LITTLFIELD and moved pensively toward it.

Chad's humble gravesite had been mysteriously transformed into a stately plot that could have belonged to some dignitary or other important person.

A concrete border had been laid all the way around the perimeter of his grave. New grass had been planted and a handsome granite bench had been set at the foot of his grave atop a layer of freshly spread black rock. We sat down together on the bench and soaked in this incredibly surreal moment. While the rain came down upon us, tears also poured down our faces. In that moment, the rain and our tears mingled down together like a healing balm pouring lavishly over our own aching hearts.

As we left the cemetery that day, I texted Chad's friend, Daron, asking him if he knew anything about this, but he didn't answer. I called Jerry, too, but he was just as surprised (and delighted) as we were.

Later that evening, Daron called. I told him the whole story of what had happened, describing every remarkable detail to him. His only reply was, "Did you like it?" With sincere Christmas joy, I told him it was the best gift *ever*!

That's when he finally revealed that eight of Chad's buddies had spent the entire weekend before Christmas working together to make it happen. Another one of their friends, Clint, had gotten on the phone with him and he told me that the group just wanted to do this because Chad deserved it.

For so many years, Chad had been the guy who watched out for others. It was just in his DNA to be that kind of person. When he was younger and single, he often became the designated driver if he and a group of his friends were out. He would willingly forego the momentary pleasures of the night in order to guarantee that those he loved made it safely home.

Another time when he was at a pool party with a bunch of other friends and their children, he was quietly sitting back just happily observing. He didn't have to be in the big middle of everything, and he was totally content to watch people around him having a good time. A child who was around three years old jumped off into the deep end with an innertube around his waist and sunk to the bottom of the pool while the party carried on.

Had Chad not been doing exactly what Chad always did, quietly observing, things may have turned out very differently for that little boy. Chad dove into the pool and pulled him out to safety. That's the Chad these guys knew and loved.

I started to cry again. These were happy tears. Tears of joy and of gratitude.

They told me that they had all pitched in, (paying for this with their own money) and that a gentleman who never even knew Chad was the one who insisted on contributing the concrete border.

Although we hadn't put up a tree or felt at all like shopping, we found the best gift we could have imagined that Christmas. It wasn't wrapped in a box or tied up with a bow, but it was made with love and would remain in our hearts forever. Just knowing that Chad had not been forgotten was the best present we never saw coming!

This curiously unexpected gift truly was our own personal Christmas miracle!

"I thank my God every time I remember you."

— Philippians 1:3

Chad carrying his daughter piggyback.

Chad's parents, Judy and Don.

Motorcycle Dreams.

High School Senior picture.

Chad and Randy White (former Dallas Cowboy).

Chad loved to go fishing.

Dale Shipman painted Chad's portrait for the Littlefield Family.

Chad and Chris with their kids at the Texas State Fair.

Chad was a descendent of Stephen F. Austin, the Father of Texas.

Chad and Daryl Johnston (former Dallas Cowboy).

Chad's first deer.

Junior High Football picture.

Youth Soccer Trophy.

Chad played for the Longhorns PeeWee Football Team.

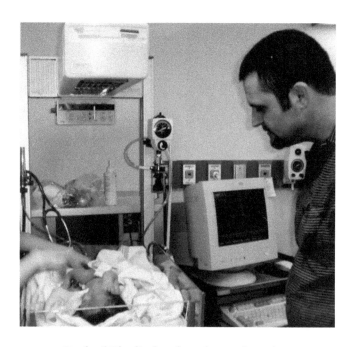

Birth of Chad's daughter, his pride and joy.

Junior High Football Broken Wrist.

Chad and his Dad at football stadium.

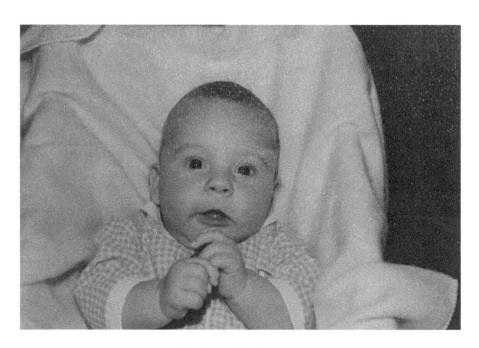

Chad's early baby picture.

Chad's parents hanging his angel wings on the Erath County Courthouse Tree.

Chad's final resting place in Midlothian, Texas.

Chad with his brother after a high school football game.

Chad and Chris.

Both of my boys, Chad and Jerry.

High School Graduation.

Chad dressing up as a Bible character one Halloween.

Elementary School picture.

High School Football picture, Senior Year.

First Grade picture.

Chapter 12

War Rooming and Battle Crying

January 2015. A new year and a lot closer to trial.

New Year's Day always held a melancholy memory for me because my dad had a massive heart attack on January 1, 1980. He had died in the hospital, unable to see a doctor because it was New Year's Day.

Bittersweet is a taste my heart knows well.

I'd never been able to make it through New Year's without reflecting on Daddy. Now, thirty-seven years later, my own son was gone, too.

The man who I had come from and the man who came from me, both gone.

The timing of things sometimes can be baffling. As fate would have it, Chris Kyle's bestselling book was about to hit the big screens in movie theaters everywhere. The *American Sniper* film release couldn't have been more commercially well timed. Public awareness and interest in Chris Kyle and his story had exploded as a result of the media attention surrounding his and Chad's murders.

The movie premiered in Dallas right at mid-January, and we had been invited to a red-carpet event. Bradley Cooper (playing Chris Kyle) and a few other celebrities would be there, and it sounded exciting. We decided to attend because we thought it would be fun, memorable, and a good diversion as we waited on more information for the trial to be disclosed to us.

So of course, the district attorney called us and said that he needed to meet with our family... on the day of the big movie event. We didn't see any reason to change anything because the meeting would be daytime, and the premiere was in the evening.

The D.A. also told us that he thought it was important for us to go over some of the details we would see and hear at the trial to better prepare us for the real thing.

There's an old saying: Ignorance is bliss. Well I can't say I was exactly *blissful* the day of our meeting, in fact, I was filled with anxiety over all the unknowns. However, I was *ignorant*! At that point, we still knew almost nothing but their names, the date, and that Chris and Chad had been shot.

Our son, Jerry, a teacher, left school at noon that day and came to the house to meet with us and the prosecution team.

Just around 1:00 p.m. the doorbell rang, and we welcomed in three people who were key players in the upcoming trial:
- Alan Nash (District Attorney)
- Jane Starnes (Assistant State Attorney General)
- Louie Laurel (Investigator)

The six of us gathered into our den. We put on a pot of coffee (the first of many), and I watched as Jane Starnes laid a large envelope on the coffee table, followed by a folder containing something that Alan Nash had carried in. My curiosity was piqued but not enough to ask what they contained. I really wanted to let them lead and tell us what we needed to know.

Two of them sat on the couch, three of us pulled chairs around the coffee table, and Don was in his recliner. We had our "war room" meeting ready to go.

The first piece of information they gave to us was that the trial date had been set. It was to officially begin on Wednesday, February 11, 2015... Chad's thirty-eighth birthday.

Time stopped for a moment, my senses went blurry, and I felt numb. Chad had been killed only nine days before his thirty-sixth birthday, Chris' memorial service had been *on* Chad's birthday, and now the trial?! It was almost too much for my mind to take in. I had to consciously choose to return to the conversation, setting aside my emotions to learn all I needed to for the trial.

The whole purpose for this meeting was to prepare us, but what could ever prepare us for this? I was prepared to be instructed and advised about what to wear and how to follow proper protocol, but I just wasn't prepared for what followed.

"We want to discuss the details of the shootings. We really need to give you this time to hear this, so you can process it some before the trial. Judy, we know your father was a mortician and you've probably seen a lot of things..."

I can't fully explain what my mind did with all the things that were being said, but I kept trying to stay with them. Slipping away and returning.

I had been born and raised in Harlingen, Texas in the Rio Grande valley. It was so close to the border that if I hadn't been a cute little blonde, I might not have been granted U.S. citizenship!

My dad was Richard Mitchell, and he was a mortician and funeral home director. My four siblings and I grew up in the funeral home because it was also our family home. Trust me when I say that we were the butt of many jokes.

Although I had certainly grown up in a unique circumstance where death and funerals and all things related were more commonplace to us than they were to the average person, there was nothing about that childhood experience that paralleled something so personal with someone I loved so dearly.

"We believe, based upon the evidence, that Chad was shot first."

My baby! My baby!

Alan Nash began to describe the injuries, "There were three shots to Chad's back and one to his side."

Dear God, no!

"We believe the defendant then shot Chris, who was defenseless because he had already emptied his rounds. We have some images here that may be helpful for you to understand the injuries to Chad's body."

He reached for the folder containing the autopsy report drawings as he asked if we wanted to see them.

My God! My God! Why have you forsaken me?

Don and I had already decided that we could not allow ourselves to see photos of Chad, but Jerry wanted to see it all. Of course, he didn't want to see it all, but his loyalty to his baby brother made him decide that he just had to take in every detail of everything that Chad had to go through.

At one point while Alan Nash was walking us through the drawings and pointing at marks on the autopsy diagram, I looked across the coffee table and realized Jane Starnes was on her knees at the end of the couch near Jerry and she was acting out what they believed Chad had done in those final moments.

It seems the fifth, sixth, and seventh shots to Chad were in his head, face, and hand. They believed he must have drawn his hands up to his face, eventually dropping his hands to the ground where his bloody handprints were later found on the wood porch of the pavilion next to where he lay dead. I guess my mind just disengaged from sheer overload and took me to a place somewhere else.

Chad had only attended one semester of college. He went and decided that he wasn't college material and told us there was no reason to spend money on college when he knew he wasn't interested in it.

As a worker, he was so conscientious and thorough that no matter what he did, he was the kind of guy who would rise to a supervisor position quickly. His tendency toward obsessive-compulsive behaviors made him a superior employee because he couldn't do anything halfway. He worked for a mobility company early on that supplied wheelchairs and scooters to patients.

He enjoyed engaging his disabled customers in one-on-one conversations, making them feel important and getting them all set up for their new lease on life he got to deliver to them as he set up their wheelchairs and scooters and walked them through some instruction. That job experience and his love for military and veterans all merged together very naturally.

Chad figured that God gave everyone two ears and one mouth for a reason, and he was an avid listener. When he had the chance, he soaked in stories from customers, uncles, grandfathers, and cousins who had served in WWII, Vietnam, and Desert Storm. He could recall all the details they had shared with him. We often found out that he had somehow magically wooed them out of their silence, and they opened up to him to speak of things that they had never discussed. Even then Chad was doing his own special brand of "talk therapy" and didn't know it.

Many times over the years when I had seen Chad's servant's heart at work, I suggested to him that he would be a great cop, fireman, or some kind of public servant. His response to me was the same each time, he said, "You don't have to wear a uniform to serve your fellow man."

I remember Jane Starnes realizing that I had caught those pieces of her side conversation with Jerry, and she abruptly stopped, got up and came to me, apologizing that I had seen and heard her.

I had already been having nightmares about Chad, picturing him lying in his own blood for hours and hours out in that field all afternoon and into the darkening night. I had been tormented by the fact that I could not go to him or help him in his last moments, nor could he be heard by anyone had he cried out for help. My heart had ached so just wishing he had not died alone.

Apparently, the shots to his back had severed his spinal cord and left him helpless until he finally breathed his last breath.

Even after those serious close calls in his high school football days, he had been able to get up and walk away. Almost twenty years earlier we had endured those fears that his spine might have been injured and he might never have walked again, yet he did. And now this. Our boy who seemed like nothing would really keep him down was finally down and there was no coming back.

Seeing this physical reenactment of my baby's final moments carried out right in the floor of my own home was completely surreal, completely unbearable, and the imagery of that was enough to torture my soul for the remainder of my days here on earth.

Jerry's eyes had simply rained down tears as he listened and watched, ingesting all this new information about his baby brother's final moments. He never cried. He just rained tears involuntarily. He had made himself view every single photograph inside Jane Starnes' mystery envelope. I'm still amazed by his strength.

Dear God, how did it come to this?

I don't know how much of that meeting I was actually present for (several times my mind had removed me from it while my body remained), but I know I returned to it at some point. They told us that one of the three of us would be needed for testimony at the beginning of the trial. Someone needed to introduce Chad Littlefield to the jury and somehow through the process of elimination, I was chosen to be that someone.

My mind was on complete information overload although there was still so much more information to be learned. I simply could not process any more at that moment in time.

This meeting had begun about 1:00 p.m., and I naively thought it would be about an hour long. Well, we were several hours and several coffee pots into this thing when Jerry asked one of the questions that came to his mind, "What should I do with my handgun when we come for the trial?" He asked because he was licensed to carry. He and Chad both had been through all the legal steps in Texas to become concealed handgun carriers with background checks, fingerprinting, and the full measure of safety protocol. He was asking because he didn't want his gun to be stolen from his truck and he knew it couldn't be carried into the courthouse.

I guess they were taken aback by his question. The district attorney told him, "You're going to see and hear so many things. Things that will make you hate. Things that will make your blood boil. You don't even need to have your handgun in the same zip code!"

Reality continued to sink in with every word exchanged that day.

He guaranteed us that there would be plenty of properly armed folks in the courtroom, so we should let them be prepared to do their jobs, and we were there to do ours as a family. That would prove to be very wise advice. We had no idea just how brutal the upcoming trial would be on our hearts.

Just before our meeting was over, Jane Starnes asked, "So are you going to the *American Sniper* premiere tonight?"

Because of all the swamp of trial sludge we had been wading through, I had lost track of time and place entirely. That part of our plan for the day had slipped from my mind, or rather it had been temporarily pushed from my mind to simply conclude the emotionally overloaded meeting.

About 4:45 p.m., nearly four hours after it had begun, we finally said our goodbyes to these fine folks who were becoming our family's team of heroes with every passing day.

We walked them out the door, as was our custom, watching them load up and pull away, and the three of us stood there silently.

I couldn't talk.

I couldn't cry.

I was virtually anesthetized, upright yet paralyzed.

In that moment, our home, our refuge, the place we felt the safest, had become the place we most wanted to escape for our survival.

When Jerry asked us again if we were going to the premiere, we decided that we needed to be anywhere *but* home that night, and so we followed our impulse to freshen up and get out the door to move across downtown Dallas at the worst time of the week, heading straight into rush hour traffic on a Friday evening, all in a desperate attempt to occupy our minds and our restless bodies. We did it with hopes of eluding an evening at home in the quiet left with nothing but our own exhausted, overactive imaginations.

After all, we had committed to attending the event, and we craved the idea of being able to escape the captivity of our own thoughts.

Chapter 13

Lights, Cameras, Action

The cold evening drizzled as Don zigged and zagged his way through the side streets of Dallas, cutting a path to our destination. My husband, the Dallas native, put his knowledge of all those shortcuts to good use, and we somehow made it to the theater in Plano, north of Dallas, with a lot of time to spare.

In addition to Don's race car driving, we had been on a roller coaster that day. We decided to attend so we could escape our emotional state, but we had unwittingly stepped off one roller coaster and onto another one of a different kind.

Neither of us really had any idea what the evening ahead of us held.

We parked the car, got out into the cold damp air, and marched bravely into the night, hand-in-hand.

Looking back, I can see how God used our ignorance and desperation to get us to the precise place we needed to be. A place we would have never chosen on our own, were it not for our compulsion to fulfill a previously made commitment.

The red carpet was literally laid out before us, and we inconspicuously slipped into the theater lobby to await an evening that would be just as emotionally loaded as our day had been.

There were giddy grown women dressed for the evening awaiting the arrival of the leading man, Mr. Bradley Cooper. The smell of popcorn and electric anticipation filled the air. The atmosphere was growing with excitement as we were simultaneously shrinking in physical and emotional energy.

We just needed to sit down, so we found some seats off to one side in the lobby, feeling a little out of place and not knowing a single person. As we sat there, we became engaged in conversation with some veterans. They had no way to know who we were and that was just fine. Blending into the woodwork perfectly suited us in our state of mind.

After they moved on, we decided to find the right theater and just go into the dimly lit room and hide out until time for it all to start. We had arrived so much earlier than we needed to, but it was worth it to us because it kept us from adding any additional unnecessary stress to our already trying day.

As we sat quietly decompressing we were also both questioning our decision to come. What had we gotten ourselves into? We still had at least four to five more hours ahead of us by the time we watched the movie, made our way through the crowd, and drove about an hour back home. Were we crazy? Maybe so, but we were there.

Just before showtime, Taya Kyle, Bradley Cooper, Jacob Schick, and a few others walked out onto the stage in front of the big screen. The crowd cheered, and the full Hollywood entertainment value of this event really hit me. As I was taking it all in, I was blindsided by what came next.

Taya Kyle welcomed and thanked everyone for their attendance and support. Then, to our astonishment, she publicly acknowledged Don and I, telling the crowd that we were Chad's parents. She said, "I want to thank these two people for raising such a wonderful son..."

At that point, I completely lost touch with anything else that may have come out of her mouth. The audience around us stood to their feet applauding. We were engulfed in a sea of love and honor. Chad's honor. One moment earlier we were a couple of invisible grieving parents lost in a crowd of strangers and the very next moment we were honored guests being publicly recognized at a red-carpet event.

Who are we to deserve such kindness and recognition?

We're Chad Littlefield's parents, that's who.

It's Chad who deserves all this love, but we're here now representing him.

I think my heart might burst!

This was such a salve to our aching hearts. The greatest fear I had was that Chad would be forgotten and God, in his generosity and mercy, was lavishly pouring out assurance to my heart in that moment. Right then, for that moment, the world was REMEMBERING CHAD.

As the famous entourage exited the stage we sat dumbfounded by the unexpected spotlight that had shone on us in Chad's behalf. Suddenly we were shocked to see both Bradley Cooper and Jacob Schick climbing the stairs through the crowded theater, heading directly toward us.

Each of these two men extended their warm hugs to me and respectful handshakes to Don, offering us kind words of condolence and sympathy for our loss.

Suddenly the long drive in the rain and cold had transformed into a gift of warmth and hope. All our doubts about our decision to attend had been dissolved into the popcorn scented air.

We had made the decision to attend out of sheer desperation, a desire to run, to escape our pain, a need for distraction. We could not have prescribed ourselves a more accurately personalized medicine for our gapingly wounded souls.

God had taken the abundance of menacing information we had received hours earlier and overshadowed it entirely with this unforeseen outpouring of benevolence delivered to us by a crowd of complete strangers, a grieving widow, and a couple of big-name stars.

Of all the places on earth we could have chosen to be that night and all the reasons we could have chosen not to attend, God had directed our path right up the red carpet and his presence was bigger than the stars of the show. Angels dressed like Taya Kyle, Bradley Cooper, and Jacob Schick had given us the V.I.P. treatment. As the *American Sniper* film began, we knew that we had not been forgotten and our pain was not being overlooked. Our Chad was not being blotted out.

Movie Entertainment???

We sat through the entire film. I feel certain that our perspective on the movie was unlike anyone else's in that theater. I tried to just watch it as a movie, but the story was just too interwoven with ours for me to be objective or "entertained."

I saw the sequence of events from Chris' military tours, but I was more distraught by the fact that one very disturbed young man had taken the lives of this hero and of my son. After all Chris had outlived while he was deployed, it was beyond comprehension that he was slain so easily, so pointlessly, and by one of his own fellow military.

When the movie came to an end Don and I sat there, paralyzed by emotion. The theater that was filled with veterans began emptying out around us.

A Vietnam veteran came and knelt on one knee at my seat. With thoughtfulness and respect, he said, "Ma'am, I know you miss your boy. I want you to know I go by his resting place often to make sure everything is the way it should be."

What?

This man of honor was right here on his knee next to me, making sure that I was okay.

Comforting ME.

Telling me that he remembered Chad often.

The kindness was almost more than I could bear. Oh, how I drank in every word, lapping them up into my parched soul and pouring them out in tears.

As we left the theater and went into the lobby, we found a crowd of people awaiting us, ready to offer us countless gestures of kindness. They loved on us, held us, cried with us and for us. We were presented with a Texas Gold Star Coin, which is a gold-plated coin. The gift was given to us by Rob Kyker, Commissioner of Texas Commission on Law Enforcement, on behalf of the state of Texas. It would become something we will treasure all our lives. I couldn't explain how a two-inch brass coin could be so priceless, but it spoke volumes to me.

With a coin in my pocket, a heart brimming with gratitude, and tears in my eyes, Don and I left that night and headed for home. It was a late night, an emotional day, and a long drive ahead, but we had focused our hearts and our thoughts on all the goodness we experienced. The highs and the lows which had all been compressed into that one day wrung us out in every way.

The only lingering pain for me that night was the fact that Chad had not been acknowledged at the end of the movie. I knew it was about Chris, and I knew the story was written and completed before Chris and Chad were even murdered. It just felt incomplete to me in that moment.

When the movie had concluded with "Chris Kyle was killed that day by a veteran he was trying to help," my heart ached and screamed out.

He wasn't killed alone!

Chad was there, too!

Chad was killed, too!

The polar extremes of all we had experienced that day stretched us almost to the point of snapping. I can't begin to describe the complexity of all we had emotionally and mentally consumed, digested, and gone through in that pressure-cooked small window of time.

Sleep.

Sweet rest.

So, my heart cried out that night.

Hold me, Jesus.

Let me rest.

The following night we had attended another premiere event at a smaller local theater. There were no movie stars, but that night the veterans were being honored as the stars. We wanted to honor them, so we attended. It was patriotic and powerful, and we were glad we chose to go.

Chapter 14

Newsworthy

We were only weeks away from the trial. After almost two full years of limbo, things were finally going to be set in motion. Somewhere in those weeks while we were counting down, we were contacted by Mr. Jon Koonsman, a writer for the Stephenville Tribune newspaper, and he was requesting an interview. It seemed he wanted to bring some of the world's attention to "the other man" who had been killed. So much of the press and media coverage had been about Chris Kyle because he was the American Sniper, so this reporter wanted to generate interest in Chad Littlefield.

With testimonies only weeks away, we had to be very careful about what we might be able to share because we didn't want to jeopardize the prosecution's case in any way. After some discussion, we determined that we wanted to partner with Mr. Koonsman so that he could highlight our son, but there had to be some specific boundaries for what we would discuss and for what he would write.

We all agreed to focus two primary things: Chad's life and our experience thus far in the loss of our son. There would be no discussion of the actual murder or the facts of the upcoming trial.

A jury had not yet been selected, therefore any new information that became public knowledge had the potential to impact or influence those who might read this article, and we had to be mindful of that important fact.

Don and I made the drive down to Stephenville again. After all, why not? Our car could practically drive itself!

I'm not sure who I was expecting "Mr. Jon Koonsman" to be or what I was expecting him to look like, but I was pleasantly surprised when we came face to face with him that day. He looked like he should be out wrestling steers or sitting on a stage singing country western songs. This unpretentious, nice-looking young cowboy put all our worries to rest the moment we shook hands with him. His genuine, kind demeanor decompressed all the tension we had carried in with us. Thoughts about the anniversary of Chad's death and all our anxieties just melted away.

We talked like old friends more than strangers. He asked just the right questions and then let us filibuster on for several hours, sharing sweet memories and verbal snapshots of our Chad. By the time we finally wrapped it all up, this Mama's heart was overflowing. There was no sweeter therapy for us than to set us loose reminiscing about our beloved son.

He took a few pictures of us and thanked us for our time.

It was a good thing he was a professional interviewer because we were amateurs, and we left there feeling like we may have utterly disappointed him with our simple stories and unpolished words.

Since we were already all the way down in Stephenville, we opted to stop in at the district attorney's office and inquire about how all the last-minute trial preparations were coming along. As fate would have it, in the short time we were in his office, he received word that the defense was in the process of filing for an emergency postponement, arguing that the current release of the *American Sniper* movie might create an unfair disadvantage for their client. They wanted to delay the whole trial *AGAIN!*

No! No! No!

Mr. Nash invited us to go down to the courtroom and sit in on this impromptu hearing. Of course, we went. Once again, in the same courtroom as the other proceedings, we sat down and waited for the judge to come in and begin.

In a short time, we were instructed to rise as the judge came in and be seated as he was seated. He happened to glance up from his papers and caught Don and I in his view. Maybe I have an overactive imagination, or maybe I'm right, but I just felt like he took one look at us and wanted to say, "How in the world do you Littlefields show up in my courtroom like this? Do you just stay camped out here?" I laughed inside imagining his thoughts, because this had been an emergency hearing.

Even the D.A. had been informed only shortly before, and yet there we sat with fingers crossed (although we lived 100+ miles away) awaiting the ruling, praying that there would be no more delays.

Once again, the goodness of God encouraged our hearts as the judge heard both arguments and quickly ruled to move forward with the trial date as planned. I can't explain the sense of relief I felt just knowing we weren't being pushed back into a suspended state. I felt like Humpty Dumpty waiting to fall off that wall again: if I fell, could I pull myself back together one more time? Now there was a specific number of days left until the trial would begin, and I could count them down easily on two hands. We headed home that day relieved and satisfied.

In the days that followed, Mr. Koonsman, the reporter, sent us copies of his completed article, just as he had said he would. I sat down with Don and read it aloud, discovering that every stipulation we had made about the contents of the article had been tastefully respected.

When I finished reading, Don looked at me and said, "I want to meet those Littlefields! They sure sound like nice people." It was a lovely article that gave us fond affection for Mr. Jon Koonsman. From that time forward we trusted him implicitly and he did several more articles that featured our journey. We knew our own flaws, weaknesses, and struggles throughout the process as well, so it was nice to read our story through the eyes of an outsider looking in. His articles were a gift to us both in that time and even now.

We now consider Mr. Jon Koonsman a very dear friend.

Living in the News World

Back at home in those last days leading up to the trial, we watched on TV as local news stations were interviewing the jury pool members who had been dismissed for one reason or another. Some didn't believe in the death penalty; others thought that the trial should be moved from Erath County because it's predicted magnitude appeared to outmatch this simple hometown crowd.

We never doubted the prosecution's ability to deliver on their end of the process, but it was still unnerving to have to trust the outcome of such a monumental set of circumstances into the hands of all these strangers.

We had a lot to take care of and to prepare for, since we did not know how long we would be away from our home—it could be days or weeks. We busied ourselves checking off all the necessary things to relieve our minds while we were away. There were bills to pay, odds and ends around the house to be done, packing, and arrangements with friends and neighbors to watch our house and to collect our mail and newspapers. All the little daily life things that add up to quite a list of to-dos to be gone without a specific return date in sight.

Even the DeSoto Police Department had graciously agreed to keep an added watch on our home while we were away due to the public nature of our comings and goings. So many people were lending helping hands to lighten our load. We normally would have preferred to be the people doing the helping for someone else, but God had a way of bringing us to the end of our capacity to force us to receive some of his goodness delivered to us by other kind folks.

Only we could carry the burden we were about to endure, so releasing those other things into the generous hands of our benevolent friends and neighbors was like throwing unnecessary items overboard from a ship entering a storm.

Our minds were continually preoccupied by the unfolding drama before us. It was, again, like reading a script that was written for a movie—except that we were the characters about to step back into story. However, there would be scenes taking place all around us reminding us that this was very much real life and the cameras were indeed rolling.

Although there would be no cameras in the courtroom, the media would be a constant presence throughout the process. We had heard that the press had been instructed not to try and engage any of the families from either side of the case or else be fined if they violated that warning. They had a designated room inside the courthouse that allowed them to run information to their respective satellite trucks outside, keeping an open line of communication to report to the rest of the world.

On the Sunday before trial began, we attended our church home to draw strength from the wellspring of prayer and support they offered us. They gathered around us and prayed for our strength, our endurance, and our stamina. A part of my heart cried out to God, just as Jesus had done before his own trial and execution when he said,

---

"My soul is overwhelmed with sorrow to the point of death... My Father, if it is possible, may this cup be taken from me. Yet not as I will, but as You will."
— *Matthew 26:38*

I would have done anything to escape the awaiting agony ahead, but I knew this was my mountain to climb and there was no way around it; I had to just keep moving forward, trusting God to meet me every step of the way.

---

*"For I am The Lord your God who takes hold of your right hand
and says to you 'Do not fear. I will help you.'"*
— *Isaiah 41:13*

This chapter of our life's journey was either going to destroy us or grow us, and I could sense the roots of my faith growing deeper and stronger, even though I didn't feel it. God was proving himself faithful to me despite my weaknesses ,and it was his faithfulness to us that sustained us moment by moment.

Monday morning came, and we loaded up to make our drive to Stephenville. Jerry drove his truck down separately from us so that we would all have a way to make a quick departure should the need arise due to some emergency back home or sickness. He had taken leave from his job at the school to be with us every step of the way. His wife, Teresa, stayed home to work and keep their household in order until a little later in the trial.

We had planned to stay in a cottage that would provide us a very private place of escape from the spotlight and microscope of the trial. It was about fifteen minutes away from the courthouse. It was close enough for convenience, but far enough out for privacy so we could retreat at the end of each day to tend our own emotional well-being.

Once we arrived, we unpacked our belongs and then drove back into town to pick up some essentials from the local grocery store. Much to our surprise and delight we unexpectedly came upon the support of the good people of Stephenville as we drove along, reading marquees and shoe-polished storefront windows that said, "We support the Kyle and Littlefield Families" and other heartfelt messages.

The people of Stephenville will never know how these gestures were like wind under our weary wings.

We spent Tuesday just doing our best to relax and rest up, trying to prepare for the upcoming week. There was so much mystery ahead of us, and the one thing we knew with certainty was that it would be physically, mentally, and emotionally sapping. Absolutely nothing could prepare a person for seeing and hearing the kinds of things we were about to see and hear. We braced ourselves, locked arms, prayed hard, and readied our hearts the best we knew how for the trial ahead.

Chapter 15

The Trial Begins

It was Wednesday morning, February 11, 2015.

Chad's thirty-eighth birthday.

The day we had prayed for and tried our best to avoid forever.

Finally.

Here.

The evidence of this impressively well-oiled machine was all around us on our way to the courthouse. As we moved in closer to the town square, the orchestration of law enforcement efforts was playing all around us.

Businesses on and around the square had cooperated in the overall effort to accommodate the unusually heavy activity by asking their employees to park a block or two further away to make room for all of us and the press. Employees gave up their regular parking spots and walked the extra distance in gracious cooperation. We were amazed and humbled by the gestures and measures extended to us all by the locals on behalf of this trial.

The court coordinator had taken strides to arrange our parking outside as well as our seating inside. We had been given a special parking permit to display in the windshield which allowed us to move through the detoured areas so we could be waved through to our designated parking. We had been instructed to call the court coordinator upon our arrival; she then directed several Texas State

Troopers out to meet us at our vehicle and escort us in through the courthouse's front entrance. All other entrances had been sealed off.

There was a large crowd of people waiting to be granted entrance and an equally bustling herd of reporters, camera crews, and satellite trucks stationed in the parking lot directly in front of the entrance.

More networks than I could name were there, all chomping at the bit, ready to snatch any little tasty morsel of newsworthy imagery or soundbites.

The feelings of both excitement and dread were bubbling up inside of me as we approached the anthill of activity that morning. I was so ready to finally get this process started after more than two years of waiting. I was also feeling anxious as I was anticipating giving my testimony on the stand that morning. If I had seen any opportunity for escape, I would have run!

As we made our way into the courthouse, we were guided through the security process. The guys had to remove their belts and shoes and empty their pockets. I had to send my purse through the x-ray machine, and everyone was scanned by a handheld wand for an added measure of safety.

They led us to an isolated area with a few chairs and just enough space to pace back and forth. The blinds were drawn to provide our small family with some privacy. The room was attached to the D.A.'s office which also had its own private restroom, so we were pretty well insulated from the frenzy of activity still unfolding just outside our cocoon.

Right around 9:00 a.m. an armed guard came for us and escorted us to the courtroom. The court coordinator had arranged our seating in advance, so when we entered there was a designated row of seats assigned for us. The law enforcement presence was very evident.

Everyone in the whole courtroom was positioned carefully like chess pieces. Each set of people had their assigned places. As we entered from the back, I could see them all strategically arranged for the impending tensions ahead.

The center aisle essentially divided the defendant's supporters (on left) from the prosecution's supporters (on right). At the front of it all were the two tables where the opposing sets of legal teams would sit with their backs to us. The jury seating was in front of them and to the right, where we would observe them as they observed the trial. Behind the tables for the legal teams there was a short wall with a gate managed only by the court bailiff. On the first row of both sides, law enforcement filled the seats, and each side had plain-clothed officers in the aisle seat. The second row on each side was filled by the press: reporters, sketch artists, and journalists, but no cameras. Our Littlefield family had the next row, and the Kyles were seated behind us. Additional law enforcement and other spectators filled the rest to the back.

I couldn't allow myself to look to the defendant's side although I'm certain his family was all nervously awaiting this just as we were.

Sobering.

Reality.

The door at the front left of the room opened and the defense team and defendant came in. Another door opened, and the judge entered. We all arose and were seated and finally the jury took their places.

All the players were present for this greatly anticipated scenario to begin.

The opening testimony was given by Taya Kyle. She was sworn in and seated. I anxiously watched her, knowing that my turn was coming. Her long brown hair, brown eyes, and brown outfit were smart and stylish, but muted. Her resolve and steely strength were loud and clear.

She tenaciously answered every question asked of her by both the prosecution and the defense. It was painful to watch and listen to her lovingly describe her fallen husband, Chris. By the time she was finished, she had given around an hour and a half of testimony that was emotionally exhausting to hear. I could only imagine how she was feeling after speaking it all, but I would know soon enough.

After Taya's testimony, the judge announced that the courtroom would recess for lunch and they escorted us to the D.A.'s office while the courtroom cleared out.

As my heart and head pounded with apprehension, I tried to quietly tuck myself into an unnoticeable corner as the tears uncontrollably flowed. I found myself surrounded by everyone trying to offer comfort and support, but I was desperately in need of solitude. Not one moment did I have to privately prepare my heart and mind for the looming task before me.

"What's wrong?"

"How can I help?"

"Are you okay, Judy?"

The well-meaning questions were rapid-fire, and I wanted to run away. I wanted to scream.

My son is DEAD!

I have to go back into that room with the man who killed him! Don't you get it?

MY. SON. IS. DEAD.

But…I didn't.

Like I had learned to do very early on in my life, I gathered my raging emotions and dutifully tucked them all back inside to fulfill my responsibility. I DID want to tell the courtroom about Chad. There was no doubt about that. I just had so much fear.

Fear of messing up.

Fear of how the defense might unsettle me with its questions.

Fear of fumbling my words.

Fear of forgetting something and missing my opportunity to do it right.

Fear of failing Chad.

Our armed escort came to get us again. It was time.

It was my turn to take the stand.

I wore black, just like the cloak of darkness that had enfolded me for the past two years. My emotions were dangerously just below the surface and I made my way forward.

Although the customary thing to do was to go directly through the gate, straight forward up to the witness stand, I had requested permission to circle around behind the prosecution table because I could not bear to be in such close physical proximity to the defendant. It was one small thing I could do to empower myself through an almost debilitating task.

Breathe.

Judy, breathe.

I was terrified.

I was so afraid that no words would come out of my mouth when I tried to speak. Or what if I spoke and the wrong words came? What if I got too hasty or got agitated and forgot names or places or things I should know to say? What if? What if? What if?

Lord, let my memory serve me well today. Please!

I feel sick.

I might throw up.

I was angry…angry that on THIS day, February 11, CHAD's birthday, I had to calmly tell the world who he *was* and not who he *is!*

Dear God! It's Chad's birthday.

I should be planning a dinner celebration.

I should be writing love notes in a card.

I should be wrapping him a gift.

I should be calling to wish him a "Happy Birthday" just like he would do for me.

I wanted to tell all about him and the sweet loving kid he was. I wanted to describe what a protector he had been and how I always knew that no one would ever be allowed to hurt me if he was around.

Oh God! I miss him!

The questions seemed unending and yet they were also simultaneously unlocking countless beautiful memories of him as I answered each one, trying so hard to keep my composure.

The prosecution showed a picture of Chad after he had caught a big fish and another of him and his baby girl... scenes I would never see again in real life this side of heaven.

I'll never take another picture of him.

I'll never make another memory with him.

I'll never hear his laugh.

I'll never see his smile.

I'll never feel his warm hugs.

Chad was gone. Never to make one more memory. EVER.

I made it!

I answered all the prosecution's questions.

I can't believe I did it.

And then it hit me. That was the easy part. Those questions were all from the good guys. Our team. They wanted me to do well. They wanted to set me at ease with their line of questioning, but I was about to face the defense. The opposition.

Are you going to try and mess me up?

Are you going to try and intimidate me?

Are you going to rattle me beyond repair?

Are you going to say horrible things about Chad and then cruelly stand back and watch me squirm?

Are you going try to mince my words or put words in my mouth?

Judy, this is for Chad.

Remember Chad.

Judy, be brave for Chad.

I had been dreading this part. The only frame of reference I had for what was about to come at me was from television and I knew that this part had the potential to be brutal.

Lord, have mercy.

Please have compassion.

Lord, give them eyes to see that I am a grieving mother whose heart is broken.

Give me strength.

I had braced myself for a hurricane pounding but God, in his mercy, brought the necessary battery of winds and rains down gently.

The defense was tempered and mild in comparison to all that my wild imaginations had conjured up. I didn't know if my mind had once again transported me to another place to protect me, but I was surprised and relieved to discover that as quickly as it had begun, it was already over.

I could only hope and pray that my testimony, which had been like an out-of-body experience, would contribute to the overall success of our cause. All I had really hoped for was that my words, my memories, and my tears would help to make the prosecution's case successful. I had hoped Chad would be proud.

As I stepped down from the witness stand it was as though my spirit and strength had been completely drained out of me through the words and tears of my testimony. I was drained empty with nothing left to give.

We were informed that the rest of the afternoon would include the 911 call and testimonies about the 911 call from the gun range immediately after Chris and Chad's bodies had been found that day. There were also supposed to be some forensics and photos. I knew there was no way I could endure listening to that, seeing that, or hearing the testimonies after my own time on the stand. So, Don and I decided to leave early and head back to our little haven at the cottage.

We left Jerry behind to catch a ride back and decided to take his truck ourselves. I wasn't feeling well at all. Guided by our Texas State Trooper escorts, we made our way out to a parking lot filled with trucks. (After all, this was Texas and in this part of Texas, everyone drove a truck.) About that time one of the troopers asked which truck we were getting in as we approached the heard of vehicles.

I paused for a moment as I realized that Jerry had recently bought a new truck, and I could not remember what kind we were even looking for! Feeling kind of silly, I said, "I'm not even sure!"

The trooper politely but light heartedly said back to me, "Well, ma'am. We need to be sure, because I am about to help you folks get into one of these trucks. If it's the wrong one, we might all find ourselves in an embarrassing situation!"

That little mishap was another one of God's clever gifts amidst a day filled to overflowing with tensions and anguish.

We had begun that day escorted in by troopers but bound up with apprehension. We walked out that afternoon escorted by troopers and relieved by our own accidental comedic moment.

The first day of trial was finished (for us) and we felt worn out, but hopeful.

Chapter 16

Happy Valentine's Day

On the second day of trial, Thursday, February 12, we got ready, headed out, and tried our best to be psyched up for whatever the day might hold. Jerry had encouraged us to leave early the first day because of the forensics and photos that were expected to be presented. As it turned out, much of those things had been delayed, so we would be sitting through those details anyway.

Firearms experts were on the stand all day. Considering I knew very little about guns, all those expert testimonies could have just as well been given in Chinese because I understood so little of what they had said. I didn't know anything about what type of ammunition was used on a specific gun. I didn't know anything about magazines or clips or safety locks or calibers or gauges. All of it began to sound very foreign and monotone to me as I sat listening for something I could grasp.

I'm certain that I began to doze off a time or two during all that unfamiliar gibberish. Who would have ever thought that all my sleepless nights would culminate into courtroom napping on only the second day of trial? Those testimonies were like sedatives.

It did seem in some ways we were relaxing into the process following such an extended season of pure restlessness.

Friday came, and the judge dismissed court early that day, leading into Valentine's Day. I guess the need to flee might have been part of the ongoing fight or flight mode we were sustaining because we had done so much preparation to be able to leave home for a number of weeks without returning, yet we determined that we would return home that afternoon to get some additional clothes and catch up on our mail.

When we got home to DeSoto and went to collect the mail from the mailbox, we were shocked to find multiple cards tucked into our box without any postage on them. These cards had been hand delivered and dropped into our mailbox by numerous national television networks looking to set up interviews. These New York City bigwigs were true to their name, hustling for the first exclusive interviews although we would be completely unable to cooperate with them because the trial was still underway. I was baffled at their tenacity and audacity to approach us during such a time.

I guess it was in those times that I was soberly reminded of just how far removed my simple life had been from the jaded world around me.

On Saturday morning we woke up after a night's sleep at home in our own bed to discover it was Valentine's Day 2015. Neither Don nor I were very interested in celebrating Valentine's Day in any hearts, flowers, or candy kind of way, but our love was very much alive and sustaining us. We leaned on each other emotionally and physically to make it through that first weekend of the trial break.

Chad was a good-looking man. Years earlier he had bought and paid for a sharp looking red soft-top Jeep. Since Chad was so fanatical about things being done well and done right, his Jeep looked like he had just driven it off the showroom floor every day, all the way down to its shiny polished tires.

One day on his lunch hour, he went through the drive through at Jack-in-the-Box. When he pulled forward to the serving window, the clerk gave Chad a slip of paper with a name and phone number written on it. He told Chad that the beautiful blonde that was in line just ahead of him had handed it to him and asked him to give it to the guy in the red Jeep behind her.

Chad called that smart girl and three years later they were married. Five years after they said "I do," they gave us a beautiful granddaughter.

Valentine's usually come in the form of red hearts and red roses. Sometimes love comes in a red Jeep.

Back inside the walls of our own home for that short day and a half or so, I reminisced about Chad once again.

He had been our Valentine's miracle baby back in February of 1977.

Don and I had married in December of 1973. Only two months into our marriage I found myself feeling nauseated in the mornings, but because I had miscarried in my previous marriage and been told I was unlikely to sustain anymore pregnancies all the way to delivery, I had dismissed pregnancy as an explanation for my sickness. When I went to the doctor and a pregnancy was confirmed, both Don and I were stunned. We were newlyweds with one child built in to the package already, and Don had no other children or expectations for fatherhood. He was a coach. Jerry plus his players were his children.

About the time we really began wrapping our hearts and minds around this idea of a baby, our whirlwind love story took another turn. A month or so into our new mindset, I began to hemorrhage. Shortly after, we found out that the baby had died in the womb.

Don was a rock of steady, faithful encouragement to me through it all. His firm and unshakable nature would be useful many times over. Just before our first anniversary in December 1974, I found out I was pregnant again. Only a few weeks into 1975, I miscarried. I was devastated and defeated, and I felt like God was enjoying playing a cruel set of tricks on me. I couldn't make sense of why God would allow me to conceive over and over only to take each baby before I ever had the chance to meet them or hold them.

I was angry.

I was hurt.

I was broken-hearted.

My body felt like it had been through a hormone tornado, and I was wrecked emotionally and physically. To top off my dark days, my doctor at the time gave me a paralyzing label and called me a "habitual aborter." What a thing to say to a woman in the throes of a series of repeatedly failing pregnancies.

Looking back now, I wonder if God was training me in some ways in preparation for things yet to come. Was he making me tough to withstand the hardest things ahead? I don't know if that's true or if it's the right way to look reflecting back, but it does somehow help me make some sense of otherwise seemingly senseless loss.

Trying to make sense out of senselessness was a challenge I would face again years later.

I never was sure how to take time to care for my heart when life just continued to barrel on ahead, but since life went on, so did we. We purchased our first home, got busy with Don's football season, enrolled Jerry in youth football, and locked our eyes on moving forward.

May 1976... I was pregnant and from the beginning I inhaled and exhaled in constant uneasiness, just awaiting a repeat of all my other miscarriages. I decided that after this baby died, I would have my tubes tied and put this horrible chapter of heartache and dread behind me forever. After three miscarriages, Don had given up hope of ever having a biological child much less a son.

Weeks became months and the months added up to a full-term pregnancy with a due date of February 14, Valentine's Day. Each day this miracle baby had stayed alive inside me growing, so had my hope and belief in the possibility of joy!

Three days early, February 11, 1977, Chad Hutson Littlefield entered this world and into our hearts. He was our MIRACLE.

He was our "love" baby.

His sturdy middle name, Hutson, was a sixth-generation family name, and he was a hearty eight-pounder who was sturdy enough to wear the name well. From the minute Chad was born, Don carried him around on his forearm. Don's buttons almost popped off his shirt he was so proud. Little did he know with all the joy that we would only have Chad for thirty-five years before he was taken from this earth.

So, Valentine's had meant much more to Don and me for many years because it was all about welcoming Chad into our lives.

There we sat, alone in our home while the world around us spun on a bed of roses and chocolates. The temporary furlough was just what we'd needed. We returned to Stephenville on Sunday. Jerry and his wife, Teresa, joined us at the little cottage that evening.

We had a week's worth of this crazy process behind us now and an unknown number of days still ahead. As we hunkered down and did all we knew to do to prepare ourselves for what lie ahead, we counted our blessings and begged for heaping helpings of mercy and grace to be poured out onto us as we faced the trial again.

Chapter 17

The Eyes of Texas are Upon Us

Monday morning, February 16, 2015 began at the courthouse in the same way the others had. We were growing accustomed to the security checks and the media presence outside each day as we parked and entered. Our armed guard escorts gathered us from our tiny waiting area that was attached to the D.A.'s office.

As we made our way to that court room I spotted my kid brother, Mitchell. What a surprise and unexpected added comfort it was to see his face. He hadn't contacted me to tell me he was coming, so he had parked several blocks away and waited outside in the line with all the others who were seeking a seat in the courtroom that day. Subsequently we were able to get him the credentials he would need to join us directly instead of moving along unsurely with the herd.

While he had waited in the crowd, of course no one was aware that he had any connection to the Littlefield family. He told us that he had remained quiet, just listening to the chatter around him. He heard someone say, "She looks better today. Not so bad." They had been referring to ME! Again, another one of my naïve little bubbles was busted as I took in the reality that not only were the people outside the courthouse observing (evening scrutinizing) me, but the cameras were capturing it all and piping it out to the rest of the curious world.

I had no idea how many people were watching. I was just a sad, surviving mother trying to keep two nostrils above the water line during this thing.

And so, the trial moved forward each day:

Testimonies.

Evidence.

Photographs.

Experts.

Guns.

Troopers.

Deputies.

Recesses.

Prosecution.

Defense.

Reporters.

Camera crews.

Some of the things presented were things we had already been exposed to during the pretrial hearings. However, all the testimonies were new to us.

One day, on my way into the courtroom, the court coordinator reached out to me and slipped a small handmade cross into my hand. One of the spectators had crafted it especially for me and asked her to give it to me to hold onto during the worst of the worst. It was such a small simple gesture, yet it spoke powerfully to my heart and it helped me through some of those horribly difficult parts.

There were plenty of times I needed something to hold onto, to distract me. I remember one particular day. The person on the witness stand began detailing Chad's murder, elaborately describing how Chad had been shot to his back multiple times yet had struggled and was still alive, so the defendant had ruthlessly returned to Chad (after shooting Chris) and shot him two or three more times in the face and head.

My baby!

My baby!

I wanted to unhear these things. I wanted to run out of the courtroom and never look back. I wanted to find a secret place to hide and scream and cry and pound my fists against the ground.

I wanted to rip the defendant to pieces with my bare hands!

You selfish idiot!

YOU caused all this!

You created all this pain and suffering.

114

You and your STUPID, STUPID choices!

Get me out of here or I'm going to lose my mind!

I could feel myself slipping, and I desperately wanted to escape this pack of cameras and reporters and random strangers who felt like hungry jackals, anxious to get a taste of my anguish.

I didn't want to comfort anyone else or answer questions or make anyone feel better about how devastated I was in that moment.

The only person I wanted to hold, or comfort, was Chad. I wanted to lean over his beautiful broken body and drape myself across him as a blanket of dignity and warmth, but that would never, could never, happen.

As soon as testimonies completed, we were quickly escorted out of the courtroom and courthouse and ushered to the parking lot. Our family stood gathered, stunned, paralyzed. We were in shock. A sizable group of Texas State Troopers remained right there with us as we fumbled with each other trying uselessly to decide what to do.

I came to awareness enough to tell my family we needed to decide what we were doing because we were keeping the troopers waiting on us. I could see beyond them all the satellite trucks and reporters probably a half block away.

One of the troopers turned to me and told us to take as much time as we needed. They were in no hurry. This band of brothers formed a wall of bodies around us and created a barricade and kept us from being exploited in our most despairing private moments. They protected our family from the prying eyes of the cameras.

That afternoon I was reminded that sometimes God shows up with skin on. Sometimes he wears blue jeans and cowboy hats, and that day he also wore guns and badges.

The whole process of losing a loved one through a violent crime had ushered so many unusual things right through the front doors of our little world. We were still ordinary people who had woken up one day to find ourselves amidst extraordinary circumstances.

I never knew where the cameras were or who might be watching. Even down to the most intimate moments of our pain. In one of these ordinary, but private exchanges, I had turned to Don in the courtroom during the trial and simply asked him, "Are you okay?"

It was a moment. That's all. Yet to my amazement, as one of my family members later told me, that whispered moment had made national news. A reporter had read my lips.

That is what it looked like to have our son's murder irreversibly tethered to the curiosity of the world.

As we rounded the corner to the end of week two of the trial, we found ourselves once again anxious to go AWOL back to our own home. In reflection now, I think just getting in the car and leaving the trial behind in our rearview mirror did something therapeutic for us. It seemed to give us some sense of control, and the time in the car for those couple of hours headed back was like a slow pressure release valve with each mile we drove toward home.

Chapter 18

We Have a Verdict

Sunday, February 22, 2015 was a cold but sunny winter day in Texas. We kept an eye on the weather forecast because Texas winters are notoriously unpredictable. The weather can go from a beautiful sunny day with spring-like warmth to an ice storm in any twenty-four-hour window of time.

True to form, our Texas weekend was turning into a threatening winter storm, so we decided to play it safe and get ourselves back down to Stephenville because we couldn't risk the possibility of being caught in the metroplex and somehow missing out on the trial due to poor assessment of the weather risk.

We made the right choice. The ice storm had come in the night and by the time we woke up on Monday morning to prepare for the trial, all of Stephenville was covered in a silvery white blanket. Snow fell on top of the ice, creating a beautiful winter scene just outside the windows of our little hideaway cottage. Storm alerts were pinging off on our phones, followed by text messages informing us that the trial was being suspended for the day due to the dangerous road conditions.

Since Jerry, Don, and I were forced to hibernate for the next twenty-four hours, we opted to use the time to gather our thoughts, put our heads together, and work on crafting our impact statement, which would be read by one of us at the end of the trial regardless of the outcome. Jerry pulled out his laptop, and we had an ice storm outside and a brainstorm inside.

By Tuesday morning, February 24, 2015, the ground outside was laden with snow but the roads were drivable, and since the temperature was supposed to remain below freezing, we weren't in any danger of new ice forming on the roads; court was back in session.

The bitter cold outside was much like the bone-chilling experience we had been enduring over the last two weeks, but just as the sun promised to shine again someday soon outside, so we clung to the hope that it would do the same over our weary hearts.

The morning testimonies were the defense's final shots at turning the jury in its favor. As the noon hour was drawing near, the judge called for a lunch recess with clear instructions that at 1:00 p.m. sharp they would begin the closing arguments.

We were nearing the home stretch and feeling every emotion imaginable as we tried to be cautiously optimistic for the outcome. Everything we had lived and breathed and had been consumed by was culminating to a pinnacle moment, and the power to affect that outcome was entirely beyond our control.

Alan Nash, D.A. came to us at the break. He wanted to prepare us a little for what we should expect.

"I know a lot of what you are going to hear during the closing arguments this afternoon will be very difficult for you to listen to, but we really need you to be in here with us. Chad is going to bring this thing home," he said.

We didn't really know what he meant that "Chad is going to bring this thing home," but we knew that he knew what he was doing and if his closing arguments were somehow hinging on Chad, we would be there no matter how difficult it might be to endure.

We returned that afternoon for the closing arguments, bracing ourselves to sit through many of the very same details we had intentionally avoided when they were originally presented.

The prosecution team would go first, which meant that the last words the jury would hear before going into deliberation would be that of the defense team. All our hopes and prayers were resting on the words and choices of these two teams. We were thankful to have such a capable team leading the charge in Chad's behalf.

As the prosecution began, we were painfully and soberly reminded that we might never know exactly what really happened out at the Rough Creek Lodge shooting range near Glen Rose, Texas on the afternoon of February 2, 2013. A multitude of experts had taken all the collective information from the scene of the crime, Chris and Chad's bodies, cell phone records, testimonies of those connected to their activities that day, and the verbal confessions of the defendant himself. There had been reenactments of what they believed to be the scenarios most likely to explain the outcome. They were confident they had come very close to understanding the sequence of the defendant's actions, even if we could never understand his true motives.

The facts that were unpacked before us in the closing arguments were unbearable. Our agony may have been palpable to the rest of the courtroom. In fact, it was probably part of the prosecution's strategy to expose us to the ugly truth as well as exposing the jury to our raw reactions.

Both Chris and Chad were found dead, each wearing guns still strapped to their hips in the holsters.

The forensics specialist who testified explained what happened according to the reconstruction and blood stain patterns he found. Chris and Chad were standing somewhat side by side and apart from each other while their self-appointed executioner was behind and between them. Chris was shooting at his target and had emptied his revolver. This madman took advantage of the moment, shooting Chris in the upper right side of his body a total of six times. He was shot at close range, never moved after being hit, and was immediately incapacitated.

Chad was shot either six or seven times. The first two shots were also to his back at close range. One of those bullets hit his spinal column causing him to drop to his knees and leaving him incapacitated as well. While Chad was still helplessly upright, he was shot to the back of his head. Based on the blood splatter evidence, he was shot again in the top of his head and face as he was lying flat on his back.

There was a wound to Chad's hand. The forensics team was uncertain but believed that wound was Chad's fleeting attempt to cover his face during his own massacre.

His bloody handprints had been found on the wooden deck of the small pavilion he was lying next to upon their discovery.

Rage.

Fury.

Agony.

Heartbreak.

Anger boiled inside me.

I can't listen to any more of this!

My precious baby!

Baby girl's Daddy — gone.

Husband, father, son, uncle, friend — gone.

Out came pictures, photographs, and images on multiple big screen TVs all around the courtroom. They were everywhere.

Chris' brother had agreed to help me when we got to this horrific part, so I turned my head toward the back, gazing in his direction as he was seated behind me and there were no TVs at the back of the courtroom. I locked my eyes on Jeff for his signal, and he watched in my behalf and motioned to me when it was safe for me to turn my head back toward the front of the room.

Every word of narrative spoken by the D.A. was like a razor blade to my heart. I felt as though I was having open heart surgery with no anesthesia and wide awake, experiencing every searing, brutal, carving word. Pieces of my broken heart were being cut out word by word as I tried not to *hear* but couldn't help but *listen*.

I wanted to escape the pain, and I imagined Chad lying there thinking the same thing, wishing for relief and a way of escape, yet getting neither.

Even without seeing the photographs, the descriptions of his death were indelibly branded into the wild imaginations of my heart.

Is this never going to end?

How much longer?

My handsome hero son and protector.

No! No! No!

It was in those moments an unexplainable blanket of awareness dropped over me, giving me supernatural peace and calm. My brain flipped its own switch, and I took a trip to a place I can't identify. I only know that I was someplace else instead of in that awful moment.

I stared at the shoes of a reporter sitting nearby.

Those look really expensive.

We could probably never afford those shoes.

Take me away.

Far away.

And the prosecution rested its case.

The time came for the defense to give closing arguments. I'm not sure if I was just so far gone by the time they presented their side, but it was somehow tolerable, even sterile. Maybe my mind was simply too saturated to absorb anymore.

It didn't last as long or feel as harsh an impact as what the prosecution had shared. Maybe the prosecution was more graphic and jarring, and perhaps that had been necessary to strategically leave the appropriate bitter taste in the jury's mouth, but I was very surprised when the defense rested its case.

It was about 5:30 p.m. when the judge called for a short recess. Don and I sat there feeling dazed and confused about this abbreviated conclusion. We had been under the impression that the trial would last probably another week longer, so this abrupt ending really took us by surprise.

At 6:00 p.m. court reconvened, and we sat curious and anxious for the next step.

The judge carefully and methodically walked the jury through a very specific set of instructions, soberly reminding them of their duty and responsibility. Afterward he dismissed the jury to go begin deliberation. They exited the courtroom with the weight of this whole case laid squarely on their shoulders.

Court was adjourned.

Huh?

Once again, we found ourselves sitting helplessly, looking for someone to gently guide us as we didn't know what to expect. I looked to our kind court coordinator for navigation and she informed us that it was simply time to just WAIT.

We wait for a verdict. The wait could be minutes, hours, or even days. There was no way to know how the jury would process all those hours and hours of evidence, testimonies, and information.

We were so vulnerable and defenseless in that moment. All our hopes for justice to be served for Chris and Chad were laid bare and unprotected as these twelve strangers carried them away in their hands to that deliberating room. We were a bubbling brew of excitement, dread, and confusion all stirred up inside.

I could sense myself readying to let down as it seemed there was a tiny light at the end of this two-year long tunnel. I was feeling grateful and simultaneously petrified with anxiety over whether the jury would truly bring justice for Chris and Chad.

One more time we returned to our tiny waiting room just off the D.A.'s office and tried to settle in for the duration, not knowing how long it might be. We were tired and hungry and weary, but we didn't dare think of leaving for any reason for fear that the jury would return in our absence and we might miss the verdict completely.

Sometimes it was the tiny, unimportant things that made this whole crazy experience tolerable. We had access to the D.A.'s private restroom, away from the public restroom out in the hallway. So many of us were packed back in that area and one day I didn't want to wait so I slipped out to the public restroom. When I stepped out, there stood several Texas State Troopers waiting on me to finish my business. I know they were there to guard and protect us, but sometimes the only way to keep my sanity was to just laugh at how ridiculous it was.

They had been so attentive to our needs, supplying us with snacks and drinks in our breakroom, escorting us everywhere we went, but the real highlight of being escorted everywhere we went was the guard dog. I assumed she was a bomb sniffing dog and each time we walked the halls from our tiny room to the courtroom, she accompanied us. She was an unexplainable ray of sunshine for us throughout the long days. Seeing her had made being tucked away in that little room bearable.

We were packed like sardines, so we took our turns marching back and forth hypnotically up and down the tiny space in our waiting room.

It felt safe like a cocoon and claustrophobic like a cell.

We waited.

6:30.

7:00.

7:30.

8:00.

8:30.

9:00.

We lifted prayers up to God, trying to release our fears into his hands, and we soaked in the blessings of the knowledge that so many prayers were being lifted for us. Text messages were flooding our cell phones with words of encouragement and reminders that we were not alone. Our hearts as well as our physical bodies were literally being sustained through this outpouring of love extended toward us by so many who cared.

Alan Nash, D.A. appeared in our room to announce to us that a verdict had been reached. It had not been days. It had only been a few hours.

A verdict has been reached?!

What?

Oh, God. Please!

Feeling a new wave of shock course through my body and mind, I collected myself and my things. We waited with both reservations and hopes until the armed escort came to walk us back to the courtroom.

As we paced down the long corridor, we marched through the troops of press who waiting along each wall. There was a sense in which we felt like we were the ones going in to receive our sentence because whatever came next was going to impact the future of our family in a huge way. We didn't know whether we would soon be shouting for joy or weeping with disappointment.

We sat down in our appointed seats once more. In a gesture of what seemed like thoughtfulness, one of the sheriff's deputies asked Don if it would be okay to sit next to him for the reading of the verdict. In truth, he was preemptively positioning himself next to my big ol' husband to manage him, in the case of an emotional outburst.

Only the twelve members of the jury knew what was about to happen regarding a determination of guilt or innocence. Once again, the tension in the air was thick and heavy. It seemed everyone could feel the weight of it looming.

Marcus Luttrell, a former U.S. Navy SEAL and friend of Chris Kyle, sat in front of me. He reached back and patted my knee and said, "Whatever the outcome, it's going to be all right."

His words and reassurance reached straight into my trembling heart. I began to cry. So much had been bottled and contained inside... it was virtually impossible to hold it in any longer.

My fears and my faith had never embraced each other so tightly in all my life. Quietly and firmly, the words of Joshua 1:9 welled up to my consciousness.

> *"Have I not commanded you? Be strong and courageous. Do not be frightened and do not be dismayed, for the Lord your God is with you wherever you go."*

I felt myself receiving that truth down into the depths of my being.

Be strong.

Be courageous.

Don't be frightened.

Don't be dismayed.

Whatever the outcome, it's going to be all right.

The Lord MY God is with ME.

The comfort in my soul was real.

Enter: the prosecution and the defense.

Enter: the jury.

Enter: the judge.

Everyone was seated.

The judge turned to the jury and asked the jury foreman if they had reached their verdict. He ordered everyone in the courtroom to remain quiet and orderly.

As the words were read aloud to the courtroom, every fiber of my being drank them in, "Guilty…Life without parole."

I don't know what else was said, and I didn't really care. What I knew in that moment was that the man who had murdered my baby boy was being held responsible for his actions, and those four words liberated my soul again! The jury had seen the truth and had rendered their verdict accordingly.

Chapter 19

We Have a Voice

Again, the judge reminded everyone that the courtroom was to remain quiet and orderly and that there were to be no recording devices of any kind in use in the courtroom. He explained that impact statements had been prepared by the families of Chris and Chad.

We had been told to expect that the defendant would most likely offer no acknowledgment or give any eye contract while the statements were being read. He was required to endure them, but he was not required to show any form of respect or contrition.

The judge called Jerry, Chad's big brother, to speak first. Jerry got up and moved toward the little wooden gate that divided the defendant from the rest of the courtroom. Armed guards stood firmly planted between my oldest son and the man who had unquestionably and savagely murdered his baby brother and just been convicted.

The words he was about to read were a collection of all our thoughts that we had collaborated on that previous Monday when we were iced in at the little cottage. It was a big moment. A moment to say what should be said to honor Chad's life, and to say it with passion and dignity.

Jerry was adamant that the statement should be fiercer than the one we had originally drafted because of all the things we had heard by then.

When the judge called "Jerry Richardson" to come forward and read the impact statement, the defendant looked up and turned directly toward Jerry, giving him full eye contact. Jerry had been one of his teachers in high school. He knew who Jerry was. Jerry knew who he was, and he knew that Jerry knew who he was from long before the shootings.

With tears and trembling lips, my handsome cowboy Jerry began:

"We stand here today as Chad's family to see justice served. Because of you and your irresponsible choices, we lost a great son, brother, father, husband, and uncle on February 2, 2013 and that will never change. Those are traits you'll never experience. You took the lives of two heroes—men that tried to be a friend to you—and you become an American disgrace. Your inhumanity and disregard for life have put you in a world from which you will never escape. Your childish actions have brought humiliation to you and your family, and they will forever have to carry the scar of what you have become. A murderer. Your claims of PTSD have been an insult to every veteran who has served with honor, disgracing a proud military with your cowardice. You wanted to be a Marine – a real man – but you destroyed the opportunity by committing a senseless act."

Jerry was courageous and composed, and his loyalty to Chad showed as well as his white-hot fury over this travesty. He made his way back to his seat. I could not possibly have been more grateful or proud.

The judge then called for Don to come forward. To our continued bafflement, the defendant also gave Don his full attention with his face turned directly to him and eyes focused.

Don was not a public speaker, and although he had doubted himself and his ability to deliver the words the way he knew he wanted them to be said, he soldiered on.

"Although Chad was not in the military, he honored and served our veterans here at home. That's what Chad was trying to do: he was trying to help you. Chad had a quiet nature and was a good listener. He cared about people, and he gave you his time because he felt like you needed it. The State of Texas has decided to spare your life, which is more than you were willing to give Chad. As much as we hurt and are devastated by our tremendous loss, by the grace of God we will not become angry, bitter, or resentful. That would keep

126

us bound to you, and you do not deserve that honor. You confessed that you did not know Chad's name when you brutally murdered him. Now you will have the rest of your wasted life, each and every day of it, to remember his name," the anguish and anger in his words cut through the air with precision like a scalpel in the hand of a seasoned surgeon.

"Let me remind you. It is C-H-A-D," Don punctuated every letter of his name, stepping a little closer and speaking a little louder with every final letter, "L-I-T-T-L-E-F-I-E-L-D."

Chad Littlefield.

My big, brave husband returned to his seat. There could never be any words that would adequately deliver the depth of our affliction or the suffering of our hearts, but we were as satisfied as we could be—that we had said what needed to be said, and we knew that the defendant had heard it.

Our hearts had been poured out in ink on the pages in those words, and the words had been mightily spoken. That was the turning point, where the rubber met the road and we had to decide how to move forward.

We had determined that we would become better instead of bitter and releasing those words out into the air was our exercise in faith. A collective, giant step toward BETTER. That was the moment we washed the demons off and set our hearts on healing.

My mind was like an interstate highway packed with vehicles of thought racing in every direction, twisting and turning, and horns blowing. It was chaotic and loud, crowded, and busy; it was jammed and congested. I could scarcely concentrate.

The jury was officially dismissed from the courtroom. We had closely watched all the jurors throughout the proceedings over the last two weeks, searching for any glimpses of how they were feeling or what they may have been thinking at different times. It had been to no avail, because they were unbelievably stone faced throughout.

Someone later told me they had seen a few of them well up with tears during Don's statement, but it wasn't until after it was all concluded and the verdict had been read that I saw the first signs of life in their faces.

I managed to capture the glance of one of the jurors and without thought or hesitation, I formed my lips and tearfully mouthed the words, "Thank you" to him. He instantly smiled a kind smile and he formed the words back to me,

"You're welcome."

That was the first moment of the whole trial that I felt like I really knew what any of them thought or felt. Very quickly the judge and the defendant exited the courtroom, and we were finally permitted to react freely. We expressed our relief in tears, hugs, and words of satisfaction among ourselves and with all the Kyle family. There was an immediate enormous group exhale in response to this positive outcome.

Our armed guard came and walked us back to our waiting room while the rest of the people there were filing out. While we waited at this late hour, we had a beautiful privilege to thank some very influential people for their contributions to the outcome. The D.A., assistant attorney general, several Texas Rangers, Texas State Troopers, sheriff's department personnel, police department officers, court staff, and expert witnesses all passed through the D.A.'s office affording us a very personal opportunity to speak and express our immeasurable gratitude.

The jury was the only group we were unable to thank face-to-face that night. They had been quietly and securely expedited from the building and away from the lights and cameras of the hungry press awaiting outside the front steps of the courthouse.

Somewhere amidst the flurry of hugs and thanks, a Texas State Trooper had come in and asked us if we would like to make a statement to the press.

From before the trial had even begun, Don and I had resolved that we would do our best to honor God in our actions and attitudes and that we would actively seek opportunities to give him glory. We wanted to remind the world who Chad was. He was the other man down, and as long as we lived and breathed, he would not be forgotten.

When the trooper asked if we wanted to make a statement, I could hear in my heart how God was telling me this was our chance to take advantage of a once-in-a-lifetime opportunity that he was giving us.

Judy, I've arranged an opportunity for you.

Are you going to be true to your word?

You said you wanted to honor me through this.

All of that happened inside my head in a few split seconds before my brain knew what my mouth was doing. I accepted the offer to go make a formal statement.

Anyone who knows me knows that I am a woman who likes to have a plan and work that plan. "Spontaneous" is not how I roll, yet the peace of God assured my naturally doubtful mind that I would have the words to say if only I would seize the moment.

I walked into the cold night air where snow and ice were still falling from the roof of the courthouse. With a protective hedge made of Texas State Troopers and with Don and Jerry flanking me, I stepped to the top of the stairway leading out, stared into the spotlights of the of the dozens of networks still hovering even at this late hour. I was overwhelmed by the mass number of them awaiting because I think I only expected to be greeting four or five of them. I was taken aback again by the reality and magnitude of the moment.

Breathe, Judy.

God give me the words.

I may get sick.

Breathe.

I opened my mouth and to my amazement, I was able to formulate this thought:

> "We just want to say that we've waited for two years for God to get justice for us on behalf of our son and as always, God has proved to be faithful. And we're so thrilled that we have the verdict that we have tonight. And thank you guys for being so compassionate and for treating us with respect and honoring us. Thank you very much."

If not for the fact that my statement had been recorded I would not be able to recall a single word of it. That, too, was somewhat of an out-of-body experience.

All I know is that when I was finished speaking, the troopers, who had stood with us, then escorted us across the way to the parking lot where Jerry's truck sat.

For the first moment in over two years, everything related to the trial was behind us instead of looming in front of us. It was probably between 10:30 and 11 p.m. and we were finally free to:

Go wherever. Do whatever. Speak to whomever.

But where do we go now?

What do we do now?

We didn't know what to do. We were like little lost lambs in the darkness. It almost felt like we were prisoners who had served our time and were being released out into the free world for the first time. We were lost.

Chapter 20

Let Us Breathe

One cognitive thought we could all agree upon was that we were hungry. Starving! We hadn't eaten all day because we had been too afraid to leave, and our stomachs were in knots, but our physical bodies were now screaming out for food.

After doing a quick search, we discovered that there was one small restaurant open late, so we piled into the truck and headed for nourishment.

In the short time it had taken us to drive from the courthouse to the restaurant the news broadcasts had begun, and when we entered the restaurant we saw ourselves on TV screens all around the room. It was surreal.

It began to make me feel a little crazy because reality and TV were becoming one. I was present in the restaurant, and I was also present in the TV. I was living both simultaneously. Between exhaustion, hunger, and unfamiliar territory, I was momentarily questioning my sanity!

Although we were plastered across the TVs all around the restaurant, no one seemed to notice or recognize us. After all we were just plain folks from nowhere special, but the media attention had made me begin to feel like there were eyes everywhere.

We sat down, ordered food, and began to eat. I was lazily playing with mine more than eating it because I was so tired. My body's need for sleep suddenly started screaming louder than the desire for food.

Our recently acquired friend and local newsman had joined us for this late-night meal and came to deliver a request from one of the major networks for us to do an early morning interview. About the time I excused myself to the ladies' room, the quiet little restaurant began to bustle with last minute patrons. They began streaming in quickly; quicker than my foggy brain could process.

As some of them began to react to seeing us there, I realized who they were. They were part of the jury. They were the only people to whom we had not yet been able to express our debt of gratitude. Lo and behold, it seemed God had delivered them directly to us right there in the little restaurant that night.

Hugs and tears were plentiful from both sides. I knew that we needed that opportunity to personally engage them, but I became convinced that it was mutually beneficial. They also seemed to be relieved to have the interaction with us just as well.

Over and over again, we thanked them using different ways to try and say the same thing, but all I could really say was, "Thank you."

We expressed gratitude to each of them for their service, doing their civic duty, for time away from their normal lives, jobs, and families, and for their sacrifice of time and thought in reaching a verdict on behalf of Chris and Chad.

Our time with them finally concluded when we tore ourselves away, promising them we would never forget them nor the crucial role the played in our family's desperate need for a just conclusion to our very unjust nightmare.

We stepped outside of the warmth of that little restaurant in the cold night air and snow was falling once again. Had it not been for Jerry's driving skills and his big Texas truck, Don and I would have been lost and stranded. Fortunately, he was confident and capable of maneuvering on the ice and snow as well as following directions out the winding country roads in the midnight hours to find our way to the venue that NBC had arranged for our interview on *The Today Show.*

We met with the production team until 2 or 3 a.m. getting familiarized with what they expected from us and then drove back to our cottage to change the clothes we had been wearing for already almost twenty-four hours. They wanted to go live at 5 a.m. in New York City, so we barely had enough time to put on something fresh. We did our best to rejuvenate, but we were fading.

When we arrived back out at the venue, the news crew had driven up from Austin with a satellite truck, and they were out playing in the snow. They were like children enjoying the rare moment of outdoor entertainment which would likely go away just as quickly and suddenly as it had come.

We went inside and were introduced to the crew who went to work setting up all kinds of lighting and prepping us each with microphones. It was clear that this was all run-of-the-mill activity for them, but we were completely out of our element. They thought nothing at all running wires down the inside of my shirt, and though I was a good bit more uncomfortable with random strangers reaching into my clothes than they seemed to be, I tried to roll with it. I didn't have enough steam left to make an issue of it, so I readied myself for us to go live in only a few minutes.

The whole interview felt off, and we were all sleep deprived and spent. We didn't know any of the questions in advance and our brains were full of sludge. We were disappointed in the way we had answered the questions and felt like we came across as naive and unprepared.

We had gone from hearing the verdict to giving a nationally televised interview in the span of eight hours or less, and it showed.

I pride myself on being put together, and I felt anything but put together; in fact, quite the contrary. I felt like we were ready to fall apart.

Returning to the cottage once more, we ached for sleep. Jerry and Teresa gathered their things and headed for home because Teresa had to get back to work. Don and I stayed for two days and took our time resting and getting our home away from home all tidied and clean. We loaded up all our things into the car one last time for a final drive back home.

For the last two years our lives had been consumed with all things related to Chad's death and the trial. It almost seemed impossible that all those excruciating months of waiting had vanished behind us. With each passing mile, we could feel ourselves drawing closer to home and life again. I wasn't even sure what "life again" would be.

It had been so long since we had just felt *normal*. I knew that we would never return to normal as we had known it before, so finding our new normal was going to be our focus. I wasn't sure if I wanted to find a new normal. Redefining normal meant accepting that Chad was really gone, but I knew we needed to begin living again. We didn't know how.

Returning home and walking into our house was like the biggest sigh of relief I had ever inhaled and exhaled. But the reality that these walls would never again contain the sound of Chad's laughter meant that every taste of sweetness would always be accompanied by some tinge of bitterness.

Learning to find our joy, a new kind of joy in a new way, now that was going to have to come from a source greater than us and it would have to include holding on dearly to sweet memories from the past while accepting that we would be making new ones in a future without Chad.

Grief is like a Shipwreck (complete)

Grief will come in waves. At first it is 100' waves.
When the ship is wrecked, you are drowning,
With wreckage all around you.
Everything floating around you reminds you of the beauty
and the magnificence of what was and is no more.
All you can do is hang on to anything that floats
while the 100' waves keep coming.

Maybe the float is a physical thing, or a happy memory
or a photograph.
Or maybe it is someone else that's floating also.
For a while all you can do is float to stay alive.
And then without noticing the waves aren't coming as
often or near as high but
they still come.

— Anonymous, 2020

Chapter 21

Life, After Death

Life has continued to give us opportunities to weave together our love for Chad with our need to move forward. Being included in things we would never have known about has become part of our healing. Each time we attend a fundraiser for disabled veterans or hear of someone who has been touched by the loss of a child or loved one, our hearts are making sense of things a little bit more.

We are discovering how this pain we never wanted brought about by a tragedy that should have never occurred is part of a future we never expected.

It's like the yellow rose exchange between Chad and me: Our first yellow rose was the result of cross words between us, something unhappy. Neither of us liked the conflict between us, but since it had already happened, we found a way to turn it into something good. Eventually, the yellow rose became such a part of who we were that he planted a whole bush of them for me.

I look back now and replay Chad's words to me about that yellow rose bush, and I can see that those are words to live by when it comes to taking care of what grows and blooms in the soil of our own hearts.

"...Mom, if you had not watered it, fed it and kept the weeds away from it, like you did for my life, neither of us would have produced."

There once was a boy whose name was Chad Hutson Littlefield.

He grew to be a man who worked hard, loved his family, and treated people with dignity and respect. His faith in Jesus was the cornerstone of his life.

He was taken from this earth far too soon, but the seeds of kindness that he planted while he was here continue to grow and blossom with the sweet fragrance of his life. Even people who never knew him in his life can smell the scent of what he left behind and whether they realize it or not, they too will be *REMEMBERING CHAD*.

> Yellow roses forever,
> All my love.
>   — Mom

Chapter 22

Memories
As Told by Friends and Family

CHAD AND HIS DAD

By Judy

Don was thirty-seven years old when Chad was born. After three miscarriages, Don had given up hope of ever having a biological child, much less a son. From the minute he was born Don carried him around in his forearm. His buttons almost popped off his shirt he was so proud. Little did he know at the time that he would only have Chad for thirty-five years before he was taken from this earth.

Family was very important to Chad. He witnessed what his older brother by a previous marriage, Jerry, went through, and it hurt Chad's heart. Jerry was estranged from his father until adulthood. Chad always appreciated his own father stepping up to the plate and raising Jerry as his own. Though Jerry and Chad were half-brothers, you would never have known that they were not biological brothers. Chad loved his dad for holding the family together, so he did not have to experience a broken home.

Chad valued the Christian support and model that Don gave. The Bible says we are not to worry about anything but in everything we are to pray. On any decision that came up Don would say, "Lets pray about it, Chad." That meant a great deal to Chad. It was Don who walked the aisle with Chad when he gave his heart to Christ.

Most kids would have pro-athletes or movie stars as their role models. Not Chad. As he said in a card, "when I think of the role model I want for my kid, I think of you." He commented that he had big shoes to fill and was so grateful that his dad was still on this earth so he could celebrate him. Chad felt so blessed.

I remember a spanking Chad got one time. It may have been the only spanking, since Chad liked to solve problems by talking things out.

Don told Chad to assume the position, which meant bend over. Chad asked his dad to wait because he needed to go to the bathroom. He went to the bathroom and slipped on two pairs of shorts under his jeans so he could not feel the lick. Chad came back, bent over the bar, and said, "Dad wait, there is a big bug on the floor." Don ignored the bug and gave Chad a lick. It really did crush Don to have to do it, but we doubt that Chad felt it. We didn't know about the shorts until years later.

Don was the defensive coordinator for the high school football team, and Chad played defense on both his junior high and high school football teams. He loved being able to go to his dad for advice about a defensive play or a question on a scouting report.

Chad asked me to mark my favorite scriptures in my Bible so if anything happened to me he would have the scriptures. Little did we know that he would be the first to share the scriptures with the Author before me.

THE GARAGE DOOR

By Jerry

Chad and Chris had a routine of working out together every day. Chris had all the equipment in his garage, so that is where they met at 5:30 a.m. daily. Those times could be spent talking and working out or silent time, whatever Chris needed that day. They wanted to take care of the temples that God gave them as well as get strong mentally and physically.

There were times when Chris would be out of town, but Chad would continue the workout regimen. On one occasion Taya called Chad and told him when he came to work out that day to come in through the house because the lock on the garage door was broken. Chad proceeded to go over and work through his routine. Before he left, he called a garage door repair man. He would do anything for anybody, especially a veteran. He would do it because it needed to be done. The repairman fixed the door and handed Chad a bill marked paid. He found out that this was Chris Kyle's house, and he wanted to give back to veterans.

It is fitting that this "Garage Door" was the opening to continue the mission Chad and Chris were doing... helping veterans.

LIFE INSURANCE VERSUS GOD'S POWER

By Jerry

It was about two weeks before his death that I had a conversation with Chad.

While working as a schoolteacher, I took a second job as a life insurance agent to supplement my income. I contacted Chad to ask for forty-five minutes of his time for my training session. Chad picked up on the questions and said, "What you trying to sell me bro?" I explained that I was not selling anything and just needed to practice and wanted to educate him on the polices. Chad was not into investments, but I had some material on investments and how scams could ruin you financially for life. Chad responded that if it was not lead or silver, he was not interested. Lead was understood to be ammo and guns. Silver was for cash as in U.S. dollars.

Chad said he would talk to his wife and set up a time to give me forty-five minutes for my training but could not guarantee that he would buy anything. I asked Chad, "God forbid, but if anything happens to you what would happen to your wife and baby girl?" Chad giggled and replied, "We will cross that bridge when we get there."

Chad did not have life insurance or a plan for a tragic event. We had planned to meet the following week, but Chad got the flu and was sick all week, so the meeting did not take place. The next week Chad was killed; I was sick that Chad was not protected.

When we went as a family to the funeral home to make arrangements I whispered to my parents, "How in the world are we going to pay for this?" It was getting more expensive with each detail we learned. My mother was determined that the family would figure it out, and we left the funeral home to pick a resting place for Chad at the cemetery. As Mom was talking with the employee about the available plots, she noticed the name of the headstone on a plot next to the one that was available for Chad. It was Chad's friend Donny, who had died suddenly; Chad was a pallbearer for his funeral. Chad also became a mentor to Donny's son. Mom and I were sure that Chad should be buried next to Donny. The lady at the cemetery wrote out a receipt and handed to my mother marked paid in full, much to our surprise. The woman replied, "Because of his service to this country." Because of the growing problem of stolen identity where individuals claim to be vets to get handouts, I responded that Chad had not served in military. She replied, "Well, he died helping veterans here at home, and that is good enough for me." Together, we fought back the tears as this act of kindness and gratefulness overwhelmed us.

When we arrived at home, there was a message that an anonymous donor had paid the entire funeral bill.

This was a great burden off my shoulders as the big brother. I felt God's message loud and clear. God was letting me know that the little piece of paper, the insurance, was not comparable to what my father in heaven covered. God showed his grace, and for that our family is thankful.

LOST WALLET PRAYER REQUEST
By Don

Chad was a strong believer in his lord and savior and the power of prayer... especially when he asked Mom, his favorite prayer warrior, to pray for him or his needs.

One day while at work Chad noticed his wallet was missing. The wallet not only contained his personal info and credit cards but also the credit cards of the company he worked for. When in the middle of a crisis, he did not have the resolve to remain calm. He knew that to find a solution to any problem you must remain calm. That was not one of his virtues. He called Mom in a panic and asked her to pray for a miracle as he explained the problem to her. He then proceeded to go home and tear his house up looking for the wallet. He went through each piece of dirty laundry, hoping that the wallet might be in the pants he wore the day before. He even went through the trash, all the time fearing what might happen if the company credit cards fell into the wrong hands. Chad's grandmother was visiting and even she was praying. He called his mom several times to see if she was praying and if she had searched her house since he was there the night before. He got back into his truck and drove very slowly back to work, checking the roadside to see if the wallet had been dropped accidentally. Upon arriving at work, he felt the need to go to restroom and relieve himself. In the restroom, he was looking down and lying by the toilet was his wallet. He checked it for credit cards and cash, and all was accounted for. Evidently it had fallen out of his pants on an earlier trip to the restroom.

Chad called his mom and said he had found the wallet, related the story, and thanked her and Granny for praying.

Most would have been too embarrassed to tell a story that had such a simple ending and asking for prayer for an everyday happening, but not Chad. He never failed to tell us in a strong voice, "Don't ever underestimate the power of prayer." God cares about anything that is a concern for us, and he answers prayers even in the bathroom.

LITTLE BROTHER NO LONGER

By Jerry

As the big brother, ten years older than Chad, I always protected my little brother. I could use my size to make a point, but if anybody tried to mess with Chad, I wanted to be there to protect him.

Chad refused to get his driver's license because he didn't need one. He had big brother to haul him around to neat places and, of course, he didn't want to work and help pay for the expensive car insurance. What a financial genius. Chad wanted to tag along, and big brother would let him ride shotgun.

After I graduated from college, I came home to reside with Mom and Dad while working at the intermediate school down the street teaching boy's physical education. To supplement my salary, I mowed yards and Chad would often jump in the truck to help.

Because I was older and bigger than Chad during the younger years, I would manhandle my little brother as older siblings do. Mom often had to intervene on Chad's behalf. She would say, "One of these days he will grow up and whip your butt." I would laugh and reply, "Whatever, we will see when that day comes!"

Fast forward to Chad's high school days: I had a yard to mow and the sweet lady offered to let me swim in her pool anytime I wanted. Yelling shotgun, Chad jumped in the truck to help me. That day it was extremely hot, so when we finished we decided to cool off in the pool. I was standing in the shallow end, and Chad jumped in, swam up beside me, and said, "Who looks up to who now?" I was exhausted from mowing, but replied, "You're still my little brother."

Chad bowed his chest out and bumped into me, knowing without a doubt that he was bigger than me. Chad was six foot and two inches, while I was five foot and eleven inches.

I said, "I am too tired, don't mess with me."

Chad let out an evil giggle and said "Remember Mom said one day I would be bigger than you and whip your butt. Well, today is that day." I was tired and just wanted to be left alone, but Chad jumped on me and started dunking me time after time under the water. I was so tired that I couldn't put up much of a fight, and Chad took his big brother that day. That was the day that my little brother wasn't so little anymore.

It wasn't long after that event that I came by the house on Chad's birthday. I was in a hurry to make plans to go out and celebrate. Chad asked me if we could go to his room to watch the UFC Ultimate Fighting Championships and spend time together. The fights were brutal. We sat down on the end of the bed and started to watch, taking in every blow that was extended and wondering how the human body could withstand that much brutality. When it was over, we hugged each other not wanting to hurt the other one. Chad said, "I can't believe we never broke anything on each other or hurt each other."

Chad was not only growing up and maturing into a man, but his respect of the dangers of human strength was increasing. His heart was becoming a caring young man. Big brother was proud of him.

FUNNIEST VIDEOS

By Jerry

The family room is where we spent most of our time together; it was a big room at seventeen feet by twenty-five feet. We could watch the console TV at one end, play board games at the other end, and not interfere with either activity.

When I came home from college, I brought Mom and Dad a movie camera for Christmas. Chad loved playing with that camera, making funny videos of his big brother, including one sitting on the throne. That video was lost when Chad did an exchange at the high school. We don't know if it got taped over with football highlights from Chad's games or if is being held for ransom somewhere.

Chad decided he would make a funny video and send it in the television show, *America's Funniest Home Videos*. The video would be of Chad struggling to climb a mountain, though it would be from the perspective of the camera.

He placed the camera on the floor and adjusted the angle where he wanted it. He laid down on his stomach and started to climb as if he was climbing a tall wall or mountain. He was making all the sounds of the struggle he was going through. He would climb some and slide down some, all the while lying on the floor and reaching for the other side of the room. Just as he was at completion of his climb, Winston, my big Dalmatian dog, walked up to the camera, checked it, out and walked up the perspective wall that Chad was using for the climb. Winston ruined the camera angle, and Chad was upset.

Some people had won $10,000 on the home video show, but Chad's chances were ruined. The incident was funny, even though the planned funny didn't work out.

In the 1980s there was a commercial on TV that enticed people to call a beautiful, scantily dressed woman. If you called, she would talk to you for as long as she could because the charges were racked up by the minute. Mom and Dad did not install cable television because it had bad language and inappropriate movies for young boys, but these commercials were out there on the regular channels. One night while Chad and I were up late playing Monopoly, this particular commercial came on TV. The beautiful lady had a phone in her hand and whispered, "Hey you." Then she said, "Come closer." Chad moved closer to the TV. Then she whispered, "Closer." Just as Chad was close enough to touch the TV, I started laughing and exclaimed, "What are you doing?" Chad was ever so corny and hilarious: "I don't know about you, but when a beautiful woman tells me to come closer, I am listening and following instructions."

DON'T TELL MOM

By Jerry

One year during Chad's Spring break in junior high he was scheduled to fly to Lubbock, Texas to visit me at Texas Tech University. Mom and Dad were driving to Oklahoma at the same time to check on our grandmother. It was before cell phones, which was a blessing for me as Chad could have called Mom and gotten me in a lot of trouble. Chad's plane was to arrive in Lubbock at 9:00 a.m. on Saturday. As most know, a college student's Friday night activities don't end until the wee hours on Saturday. I woke out of dead sleep on Saturday morning, looked at the clock: 11:00 a.m. I jumped up, put on some clothes, and drove like a race car champ to the airport. Once the car was parked, I went running into the Southwest Airlines luggage claim area and spotted Chad with a look of disappointment on his face. His strong work ethics had kicked in. He was behind the counter helping the Southwest attendant tag luggage and put it on the conveyor belt to be loaded on the plane. I saw him and ran to him wondering what he was going to tell Mom. The first words out of my mouth were, "Don't tell Mom."

I was excited to see my little brother and show him what Lubbock had to offer. I had planned places to take Chad, one of which was the Estacada Winery. The tour explained how the wine was made, and at the end of the tour the associates showed the tourists how to look for rings as they swirl the glass, smell the aroma of each glass, and appreciate the art of making a fine wine. The samples were abundantly lined up along the bar. As I was swirling the glass and smelling the aroma, I looked back at Chad who had skipped all the steps of tasting and was drinking the glasses of wine like they were shots of whiskey—like he was a cowboy in a western movie. Halfway through the samples Chad was inebriated. I was safe for being late at the airport because when Chad vomited up his intake, he said, "Don't tell Mom." I didn't know if Chad was impressed with what Lubbock had to offer, but brotherly loyalty was certainly established.

LAND SLIDING

By Jerry

Chad never came across as a crazy adventurer when you saw him hanging with his friends. He didn't ride bulls or broncos in the rodeo like his friend Chris, but he was, as they say, funny and crazy enough to try something new.

There was a time Chad came into the kitchen to visit and talk while Mom prepared the dinner we would enjoy that evening. As they were talking, I looked at Chad's arms and noticed road rash all over them. I thought Chad had reverted to his kid days when he totaled his new bicycle he got for his birthday. "You still haven't learned to ride your bike," I said to Chad, who laughed it off.

When Chad was about seven or eight years old, he got a new bike for his birthday because he finally learned to ride without the training wheels on his small bike. He and a neighbor were on their bikes barreling down the alley at a great rate of speed. Mom, Dad, and I were sitting on the patio surrounded by a fenced yard. Suddenly we heard a loud crash and the anguished cries of Chad and his friend. The three of us looked at each other and as a choir together we sang out, "What was that?" Moments later screams of terror came from the other side of the fence. We all ran for the side gate and saw Chad with blood running from his chin down to his chest and hands. He had been riding with no shirt on. When their bikes collided, Chad was knocked off and proceeded to slide across the concrete alley. The new bike was a mangled mess. The seat was turned and torn. The handlebars were completely of their sprockets. Mom ran to his side to rescue him, and I was in shock thinking that is going to leave a bad burn if we ever got the gravel out of his skin. Dad, on the other hand, took on his high school coach mode and yelled at Chad for tearing up a brand-new bike. We laugh at that moment now as Dad felt bad about his initial observation of the situation. We guessed that Chad had not quite learned to master the brakes of the new bike and thought flying over the handlebars like Superman without a shirt would give style points with his stop. My response and remarks to the crash were not funny to Chad.

Back in the kitchen, I asked about the scars on Chads arms and he replied, "Land sliding." I said, "What in the world is that?" Chad seemed to ignore me and asked Mom how long it would be until dinner. "It will be a while," she replied. With a smirk, Chad said to me, "Let's get in your truck, and I will show you." We drove out to a vacant field where we saw some of his friends congregating and taking turns on this newfound sport. While I watched those crazy kids do the unthinkable, Chad smiled and with a tough voice said, "We invented this game." These boys took an old knee board—the kind you pull behind a ski boat—attached the rope to the bumper of a pickup truck, and rode the grass behind the truck, sliding across the pasture as one would a lake. Chad looked at me and said, "Land sliding." Despite my protests of this "sport" as crazy and dangerous, Chad insisted that it was fun. "Do you want to try it?" I blurted out not no, but hell no. Chad said the road rash on his arms was when he wiped out, rolling across the field when he fell off. Chad did some crazy things, and now I when look on ESPN and see these extreme sports, I think about Chad and his friends inventing extreme sports before it was popular.

FIRECRACKERS

By Steven Day

As I look back in my memory of all Chad and I shared, it's strange to think it all happened within a span of about six years. He was a staple of my coming-of-age years from twelve to eighteen, and every major milestone I can remember has his grinning face in it. A million moments, a thousand adventures, one exciting memory after another and it has been so hard to recount just one stand-out moment. Which one do I pick? The funniest moment? The craziest adventure? The most endearing? It's so hard to decide. For me, Chad *was* my childhood. My children, who are now eighteen and thirteen, have grown up hearing Chad's name on a regular basis. There are precious few moments of their childhood I could not connect to my time with Chad. He would always come up and my kids would hear, "This one time me and Chad..." and off I would go recounting some crazy and adventure as my kids listened with wide eyes and ears.

Our home lives were quite different; I moved a lot and was raised by a single mom, and so there always seemed to be something going on at my house. As a matter of fact, it became a common phrase he would use, "Always something going on at Steven's house." Little did Chad know it was likely the fact he was there which made the adventures happen. I guess if I were to recount one story that stands out in my memory, I would say the one when we were probably thirteen. The house I lived in had a double-car garage, but the entry consisted of two single car doors separated by a column.

One summer night when he was spending the night with me—we were always at one house or the other—we had only one of the doors open and there just happened to be two couches stored in the garage. Well, we had the house and the evening to ourselves, and so we thought it would be fun to take bang snaps (gunpowder wrapped in white tissue paper) and place them out on the street for cars to run over them. What else do thirteen-year-old boys do in the suburbs on a warm summer night? Well, we had the process down pretty good. We would run out to the road, place the bang snaps, run back to the garage, and lay on the couches to peek over the arm rests, waiting and watching. When the cars would run over them, we would laugh and say "Awesome!" while thinking very highly of ourselves and our rebellion.

One time Chad stayed on the couch, and I ran to the street and started placing bang snaps when all of a sudden a car came flying around the corner, literally squealing the tires a bit. Although I was caught within the light beams I bolted for the garage. As I ran into the garage the vehicle proceeded to pull into the driveway, lighting up the inside of the garage with Chad still laying of the couch. I didn't stop but ran into the house shutting the door quickly behind me hoping I had done it fast enough to have not been seen by the car. I went out the back door where I could still see the lights of the car shining and stayed put until it pulled out and drove away. Heart pounding, I ran back to the garage and found Chad grinning from ear to ear wondering what in the world that was about. We calmed down, laying on the couches talking and laughing and starting to assume that our adventures for the evening had come to an end; suddenly lights pulled into the driveway once again, and this time we were both in the garage. We heard car doors open and suddenly more light flooded in, this time moving as if coming from powerful flashlights. We heard footsteps coming closer and closer. We both froze. Laying on the couches still as stone, it was clear that there were two men with flashlights standing at the entrance of the garage.

Suddenly Chad, being the braver of us, sat up quickly and shielding his eyes from the blinding light, said "Hello??" To our dismay it was two uniformed police officers! And the vehicle was a patrol car with the spotlights turned on! We got a little talking to by the cops about running in and out of the street on a dark night. As it turned out, I had a police officer neighbor who wondered about the suspicious activity and had called his friends to come check it out. Of course, Chad, as cool and smooth as ever, grinned and said lots of "Yes, sir" and "No, sir," and they got back into their patrol car and drove away. We both stared at each other in amazement. "Always something going on at Steven's house!" What better memory for a couple of teen boys! Playing with explosives, almost getting caught by the cops, home alone with no adult supervision... we were regular rebels, bad ass tough guys.

It was Chad who made moments like that so memorable, so exciting—and he always knew what to do. I always knew I was safe with Chad. I always knew that no matter what came up, if he was there everything would somehow be okay. If his dimples and grin didn't get us out of it, surely his mouth would. I could fill a book with stories just like this one that would speak to so many of his qualities, but it's stories like this that represent the innocence and wonder of my childhood, that shaped me into the man I am now. Without Chad in them, I would be an entirely different person and certainly far less than the man I am. I will never be able to effectively express my gratitude for my years with him. He showed up in my life just as my parents were divorcing; dispatched by God himself to be a pillar, a comfort, and a source of great joy my heart so desperately needed. My life was never the same once he stepped into it and although his absence now leaves a gaping hole, his memory and our time together will live on forever in my heart. I love you bud; I'll see you again soon, and we will share new adventures together.

WORDS FROM A FRIEND'S MAMA

By Vickie Day

When I first met Chad, I was instantly in love with this kid. He was personable, always smiling, and always on the verge of getting into trouble. His kind of trouble was usually pulling pranks. I remember taking him and Steven to the mall (big mistake) only to have them act out and yell "Mama!" from the other side of the store! If I acted as though I was embarrassed, Chad would hang on me and say, "Mama, what's wrong! Do you love me, Mama? Oh, have mercy!" When we would get in the car, I would threaten them with bodily harm, and Chad would just laugh and tell me it was all going to be all right. He always rode his bike wide open, not even slowing down as he would reach our yard, jump off his bike, and trot to the front door without missing a beat. Always smiling as he said, "Hi Mrs. Day, is Stevie here?" He was Mach 10, full throttle all the time. When he went home, I would be exhausted because he insisted you engage with him and his complete love for life. He was forever telling me not to worry, that everything was going to be all right. When he was around, I believed it.

We moved away to New Mexico, and my son stayed in touch with him for a long while. Then he came out to visit us. I love to cook and was just what Chad had hoped for. His requests seemed endless and, as I recall, I fulfilled them all. He kept us laughing, and I realized then that the little boy I had known had grown into a wonderful young man, but he had not lost any zeal for life or for pulling pranks. One of the last conversations Chad had with me was the day before he left. He had been telling Steven that he needed to keep his room cleaner. I walked in the room and told Chad how I appreciated him encouraging Steven to do a better job with his room. He said, "Don't worry, he'll do better, but you will have to stay on him because he had rather play video games."

Oh, the things I would have said to him if I had known that this would be our last conversation. I am so glad he came into my world even if it was so brief. I know without a doubt if I could talk to him, he would say "Don't worry, everything is going to be okay." Because of you, Chad, I still believe it.

MEMORIES

By Chris Knight

I can't remember which kid's birthday it was—it may have been his daughter's.

There was a blow-up swimming pool in the back yard, I was late getting to the party and when I walked out the back door, all I could see was a bunch of kids playing in the pool along with Chad lounging in it like he was at the Hilton.

Most evenings the guys on the street would go out to a neighbor's house and shoot hoops. It never failed that after being out a while, here would come Chad strolling down the sidewalk wearing his Crocs, walking with a little swag, stopping at the end of the driveway, and say, "Wud up dogs." Just like he was going to shoot hoops in those silly Crocs.

The night Chad and Chris were killed, us guys met across the street from Chad's house in another neighbor's driveway. We stood there in silence for what seemed like years in the cold February air, not knowing how to feel. We eventually started trying to figure out how to take care of his family and protect them from the media and all of the things we knew were to come.

You shouldn't have to do that for your friend. You should be shooting hoops and having fun. We were at a loss for words. That was one of the hardest nights of our lives.

MEMORIES

By Mallory Horton

My family moved from Arkansas to DeSoto, Texas when I was about ten. We moved into a trailer park in the area. I had made a few friends there, but I had anxiety about going to a new school and not having any friends. I was a very awkward kid at that age because I was a bit bigger than everyone. To hide my loneliness and awkwardness, I went to the corner of the playground where the merry-go-round was to stay out of the way. There was another kid sitting there. He had no fear and the first words out of his mouth was, "Who are you? You were not here last year." His name was Chad Littlefield. He was wearing what I call today his "Chad face."

From that moment on, Chad took me under his wing and introduced me to everybody in school because he knew everybody. Chad always had a kind, generous heart.

After playing a few years of youth football together, we graduated to junior high sports. We were both good because of our size compared to the kids at that age. There were two junior highs (called middle schools now) in our town, and football season was a big rivalry. It was like the Super Bowl to us. We spent the week before getting ready for the big game with the full attention of the cheerleaders and the backing of the entire school. On the morning of the game, after the pep-rally, the football team met in the locker room with the coach. Coach talked with us to get us fired up before the game. Chad got so excited and fired up that he slammed his fist into the locker door. The result was that Chad broke his wrist and missed playing in the game. Coach let him suit up and stand on the sidelines but no game for him, and no one was allowed to hit a locker with their fists again.

Keeping with football, our sophomore year Chad had a great Spring season and was named the most improved player. He had all the scrimmage films from the Spring games. One day I went in his room when he was not there and watched all the scrimmages. When I stopped the varsity scrimmage video I must have hit the wrong button or something. The next day when I saw him, he said the whole dang video was erased. Needless to say, he was not happy. I stayed away for about a week. He had won the most improved player, and I had erased all the proof of it.

The ultimate story is when Chad met his wife and married. Five years later they had his daughter. I really saw him change before my eyes. Chad became one of the best men I have ever known. He would call me several times a year to check how I was getting along. I am notoriously bad at staying in touch with people, and he always made sure we did just that. In fact, one night Chad called me to come have a beer with him. I didn't know until I got there that Chris Kyle was with him. Meeting Chris was cool, and we told more than a few stories.

Chad was a great friend, and great friends come from great families. I cannot tell you how much Chad and his family have meant to me. Hell, along with other families, the Littlefields practically raised me. I hope these stories give you a little insight about what a good man Chad was.

A SERVANT'S HEART

By a former co-worker

On April 3, 2012, a tornado touched down south of Dallas. Chad had been listening to the radio in his employer's warehouse when the emergency weather alert came over the airways. Chad proceeded to the office and helped escort each employee to a safe place. When he was sure all were safe, he went to the warehouse doors and watched the tornado lift over the building and then come down again in a near-by city, eventually hitting a trucking company and tossing truck rigs twenty feet into the air. He had wanted to ensure that everyone was safe, but he did not want to miss any excitement.

At the time of Chad's death, he was logistic manager of a water treatment company. He suffered from obsessive compulsive disorder. He was never diagnosed as such, but to those who knew him it was clear. Because of this disorder he was overly organized. His theory was if it did not have a place, you did not need it. It was hard for him to delegate because no one could do it as well as he could. His workplace was immaculate, and the company trucks were spotless. He always had his phone close by in case his employer or customer needed help. His employer told me that Chad could not be replaced. They would try and train another, but there would never be another Chad.

Another coworker and good friend of Chad's shared a story and photo with me in the days that followed Chad and Chris' death. It was of two doves that sat together on Chad's office window all day long. Was it a coincidence? I don't know, but it was an odd happening.

A LOYAL FRIEND
By Chelsea Edge

This one is my favorite stories because it shows exactly the kind of friend I had.

We each got married and started having babies about the same time. Although we still talked, our conversations were fewer and we rarely saw each other during this time because my family moved further north, and he moved further south. We just got busy with navigating our new lives.

One day I went looking for a friend of ours who I recently found out was a photographer. I needed pictures of the kids done, and so I called Chad Bailey... at least I thought I was calling Chad Bailey.

Me: Hello? Chad—It's Chelsea, how are you?

Chad (Littlefield): Chelsea?!

Me (confused): Ya (pausing waiting for response... none, so...) Chelsea Edge...Married to Justin?

Chad (also sounding confused): Ya, I know who you are married to... just surprised to hear from you. It's been a while!

Me: Well, I'm calling because I needed pictures taken of the kids, and I was wondering if you would do them?

Chad (sounding more confused): Well okay... where and when were you thinking?

Me (I'm confused why he is sounding so confused now): I was thinking at the Arboretum—what do you think?

Chad: Okay, sure, what time were you thinking... I may have to come straight from work. I get off around 3:30–4:00. I may be in work clothes. Is that okay?

Me (why is he coming from work—isn't he a photographer? Work clothes??): Well... okay? I can meet you at four at the Arboretum, I don't care what you wear (now regretting asking this guy, clearly not a professional).

Chad: Are you going to bring your camera, or do you need me to bring one?

Me (he needs me to bring a freaking camera?!): Oh... Do you not have one you use? I have one but it's not very good?

Chad: I mean I can stop and buy one, or get one of those disposable ones??

Me (what in the world?!): Wait!!... Chad? Is this Chad Littlefield???

Chad: Uuh... Ya?

Me (laughing hysterically): I thought this was Chad BAILEY! Can you imagine if I would've shown up with my kids spending all that time getting picture "ready" and finding you with your disposable camera ready to take my kids pictures (laughing so hard). Why didn't you ask me why I wanted YOU to take the pictures???

Chad (also laughing): I just thought, poor thing, maybe she has had a hard time making friends and just needs someone to take her kids' pics. I was just as confused as you were!!

Me (still laughing): Oh gosh Chad you are so funny! I miss you, and you're partially right... I don't have friends as good as you. You are the best!

Chad (giggling): It's good to hear from you. Let's get together soon...

The conversation trailed off into how are yous, and what are you up tos. He hung up and called Justin right after. This is also how they reconnected, deciding to drive to Austin and got another tattoo together.

Moral of the story: My friend was willing to go out of his way to take pictures of my kids, even with a time getting in our way, he was still a sweet and loyal friend to me.

Things I remember about Chad as my friend:

- He hated you to sit on his bed and mess it up... so we did just to bug him.
- He had fifty pairs of tennis shoes, kept neatly all in a row.
- He hated a party. We could not drag him if we tried. We would say we were going out and his first question would always be... how many people are going to be there and/or who is going to be there? He would follow up with, "I'll catch up with ya'll later."
- Kept his Jeep spotless.
- Gave the best hugs.
- Had the best giggle.

MY CAR IS MISSING

By Norma Todd

I was Chad's high school teacher and one day after school I went to the parking lot to get into my car and go home, only to discover that my car had disappeared! A bunch of boys, Chad included, were standing nearby and they were all laughing. I was starting to think the worst, when the boys started to giggle and act really strange, pointing and jumping around. They finally admitted they had picked my car up and carried it to the other parking lot! I never knew who instigated the prank, but I strongly suspected Chad. I loved that they liked to pick on me, and I've never forgotten.

NUMBER ONE CHAPERONE

By Norma Todd

Chad and my daughter Lauri were friends from kindergarten all the way through high school. They used to walk to school together when they were little. As they grew up, they ran around together, along with of bunch of other kids. Lauri was a cheerleader, and Chad played football. On Friday nights after the football games, a bunch of these kids would gather at our house to eat, dance, and play games. Occasionally, the kids wouldn't go home and would eventually fall asleep on my playroom floor. I never left the kids unchaperoned, so one night, I was tired and laid down on the playroom floor, too. Chad was the kid closest to me so I put my hand on him so I would wake if he tried to get up. The next Monday at school, everyone was laughing, and someone came in my room and told me that Chad had informed the coach and the team that he had slept with Mrs. Todd! We all had a good laugh. He had such a wonderful personality.

I was also one of Chad's teachers in junior high. He made me smile and was never disrespectful and always kidding with me. In later years we attended the same church that Chad and his family attended. My husband and I sat near them during the service, and he always sought me out to give me a hug. I loved Chad and miss him.

ACKNOWLEDGMENTS
FOR ACTS OF KINDNESS

The back room in our house, which was once Chad's bedroom, we now use as an office. It has become a room filled with tokens of comfort. So many of the tangible expressions of kindness that we have received now have their home in that room. It's my pleasure to use the remainder of the pages of this book to share some of the beautiful gifts we have received, most of which have come from people we would never have come to know were it not for the tragic way Chad died. Even the memory of his murder has become wrapped in the warmth of the loving expressions offered to us by many a kindhearted stranger.

SENATOR BRIAN BIRDWELL

Senator Birdwell is a survivor of the Pentagon bombing on 9/11. He endured severe burns as he was working that day in the Pentagon.

We met the Senator and his wife, Mel, when we were invited to the Texas State Capitol for the resolution that was presented in Chad's honor. We met with the Senator prior to the reading of the resolution on the Senate floor. He presented his challenge coin to each of us. After the reading, he presented us the Texas flag which had flown over the capitol on the day Chad was buried. He has been instrumental in keeping Chad's memory alive, mentioning him every time he talks about Chris Kyle. Thank you to the good senator and his dear wife, Mel, for all you do.

PATRIOT GUARD RIDERS MOTORCYCLE ESCORT

The Patriot Guard Riders is an organization of motorcyclists who escort the bodies of veterans to their final resting places. We were told that they broke precedence by escorting Chad, who was a civilian. They explained that they chose to because, "Your son, our hero, died serving America's veterans—all of them." Although it was outside of their protocol, there was never a question as to whether they would escort Chad. Their whole troop rode from the funeral home to the church, and then created a human barricade at the church parking lot, preventing the press from imposing on the family's ceremony. After the service, they escorted Chad's body to the cemetery. They promised me that Chad would never be forgotten.

Ride on PGR! What a blessing your kindness has been.

SAMMY L. DAVIS
Congressional Medal of Honor Recipient Challenge Coin

I had the honor of meeting Mr. Sammy L. Davis at an event sometime after the murders. Several weeks prior to their deaths, he had seen Chris and Chad somewhere, and we discussed how Chad had been in awe of his Medal of Honor and had asked if he could touch it. A Congressional Medal of Honor is the highest award a soldier can receive, given only by the President of the United States and only for life-saving acts that are beyond the call of duty.

Sometime during the event, as dinner progressed, a tribute was given for "the missing man," which is for soldiers who do not return home. Tears streamed down my face as I related our loss of Chad to these that were being honored. He was our missing man who never returned home. Across a dimly lit ballroom, Mr. Davis noticed my tears and made his way to me, saying, "Mrs. Littlefield, I need a hug."

I responded to his kindness, saying, "I need one, too."

He told me he had given Chad one of his challenge coins, but then went on to offer me one also. He told me he wanted me to have one in my possession just in case the one he had given Chad didn't make it to me.

Mr. Davis, your kindness will never be forgotten.

DALE SHIPMAN
Chad Littlefield Portraits

I had seen some of Mr. Shipman's pencil drawings on Facebook, and I made contact with him to inquire about his pricing because I was interested in having a drawing made of Chad. After hearing how Chris and Chad were murdered, he felt compelled to gift us with a pencil drawing of Chad as a condolence for our loss. We drove to Tulsa, Oklahoma to pick up this beautiful gift and were so humbled by his unsparing benevolence. He told us that we had already paid the ultimate price, and he decided to surprise us with a full-size oil painting of Chad as well. The oil painting hangs proudly on the wall in Chad's old bedroom. I see him every day when I go in that room to work.

Mr. Shipman, the beauty of Chad's portrait is paralleled only by the goodness of your giving heart.

JUSTIN SMITH
American Flag

From December 4, 2015 through January 3, 2016, a Special Operations MH-47G Chinook helicopter carried an American flag on board as it completed multiple missions abroad. Staff Sergeant Justin Smith was on that MH-47G and told us that the flag was carried with pride and honor in remembrance of Chad Littlefield (who paid the ultimate sacrifice for his fellow man). That flag bore witness to unspeakable acts of bravery and heroism as well as 100% success on all the classified missions undertaken while it was on board. Justin presented the flag to us accompanied by a certificate of authenticity. What a day of rejoicing it was when we received that flag. It now hangs in our home as a tribute to Chad.

The words "Thank you" are not enough, Justin, but it is the best we have to offer in return for the significance this gift.

RICK AND TANCY TURNER

We had the good fortune to meet Rick and Tancy Turner at a motorbike race. Rick invited us to attend their annual gala, "Spirit of a Hero," where Noah Galloway was going to be speaking. At that time, Noah, a double amputee, had recently finished as a contestant on the hit television show *Dancing with the Stars*. Our granddaughter was a big fan of his and could hardly wait to meet him. Circumstances did not allow for her to attend, so Rick worked out the details to get Noah to sign one of his books, *Living with No Excuses*, and inscribe a personal note to her. Chad's daughter could not have been more thrilled! Weeks later, I contacted Rick to get information on how to go about having memorial coins made in Chad's honor, and he quickly asked me if I trusted him enough to let him handle the details, and I was delighted that he made the offer. A few months later, we met them for dinner and were given a box of shiny new memorial coins bearing Chad's image. One side of the coin reads, "2-11-1977 Chad Littlefield 2-2-2013, Never Forgotten" and on the other side bears a Texas flag, "A Warrior Amongst Us and a Loyal Friend."

Thank you, Rick and Tancy. You have left an indelible imprint on our hearts and lives.

This list is but a small reflection on countless kindnesses shown to us since Chad's death. The fog that accompanied his traumatic death makes it impossible to remember all of the things which were done for us, given to us, and offered to us during the days, weeks, and months that followed. All we know for sure is that this list of people is merely representative. The gifts they gave to us have impacted our lives for good and enabled our grieving process to move forward. We know that Chad has not been forgotten.

ABOUT THE PUBLISHER, TACTICAL 16

Tactical 16 Publishing is an unconventional publisher that understands the therapeutic value inherent in writing. We help veterans, first responders, and their families and friends to tell their stories using their words.

We are on a mission to capture the history of America's heroes: stories about sacrifices during chaos, humor amid tragedy, and victories learned from experiences not readily recreated—real stories from real people.

Tactical16 has published books in leadership, business, fiction, and children's genres. We produce all types of works, from self-help to memoirs that preserve unique stories not yet told.

You don't have to be a polished author to join our ranks. If you can write with passion and be unapologetic, we want to talk. Go to Tactical16.com to contact us and to learn more.

CPSIA information can be obtained
at www.ICGtesting.com
Printed in the USA
JSHW031232150920
7928JS00004B/20